CW01334900

# *The Vine Manual*
*Instructions for the Cultivation of the Grape Vine*

## by Journal of Horticulture

**with an introduction by Roger Chambers**

*This work contains material that was originally published in 1879.*

*This publication is within the Public Domain.*

*This edition is reprinted for educational purposes
and in accordance with all applicable Federal Laws.*

*Introduction Copyright 2018 by Roger Chambers*

# COVER CREDITS

**Front Cover**
*Ripe Grapes* by Scott Bauer *USDA / Agricultural Research Service*
[Public Domain],
via Wikimedia Commons


**Back Cover**
*Wine and Grapes from Above (unsplash)* by Roberta Sorge (robertina)
(https://unsplash.com/photos/IywM7AQTZcM)
[CC0 – Universal Public Domain Dedication],
via Wikimedia Commons


**Research / Resources**
*Wikimedia Commons*
www.Commons.Wikimedia.org


Many thanks to all the incredible photographers, artists,
researchers, biographers, historians, and archivists who share
their great work via the Wikipedia family.


**PLEASE NOTE :**
As with all reprinted books of this age that are intended to perfectly reproduce the original edition, considerable pains and effort had to be undertaken to correct fading and sometimes outright damage to existing proofs of this title. At times, this task can be quite monumental, requiring an almost total rebuilding of some pages from digital proofs of multiple copies. Despite this, imperfections still sometimes exist in the final proof and may detract slightly from the visual appearance of the text.


**DISCLAIMER :**
Due to the age of this book, some methods or practices may have been deemed unsafe or unacceptable in the interim years. In utilizing the information herein, you do so at your own risk. We republish antiquarian books without judgment or revisionism, solely for their historical and cultural importance, and for educational purposes.

# Self Reliance Books

Get more historic titles on animal and stock breeding, gardening and old fashioned skills by visiting us at:

# http://selfreliancebooks.blogspot.com/

# introduction

Here at **Self-Reliance Books** we are dedicated to bringing you the best in *dusty-old-book-knowledge* to help you in your quest for self-sufficiency and food independence.

We're so pleased to bring you another title on Horticulture – this time a wonderful old gem on growing Grapes. With such a versatile crop that can yield everything from wine and juice, to raisins and jelly, the Grape is a fabulous crop to grown in your Back-Yard Orchard.

This special edition of **The Vine Manual : Instructions for the Cultivation of the Grape Vine** was published by the *Journal of Horticulture* in 1879, making it just shy of one-and-a-half centuries old.

The book features sections on *Soil, Borders, Choice of Plants, Varieties of Grapes, Planting, Pruning*, and more.

This interesting old text is a great addition to your historical horticulture library, and a must read for all those interested in the history of Grape Culture.

~ *Roger Chambers*

*State of Jefferson, April 2018*

# PREFACE.

MANY representations have been made to the Editors of the "Journal of Horticulture" that a work of moderate cost is needed, treating of all the methods of cultivating the Grape Vine. With the view of meeting this need the present volume has been prepared, and as it contains no instructions but those which have been furnished by some of the best practical gardeners, it is confidently offered as a trustworthy guide.

# THE GRAPE VINE.

THE Vine is an accommodating plant, easily grown, and very soon bears fruit In this country it is grown against walls without any protection, but with more certainty and excellence if with a glass covering; in orchard-houses, in greenhouses, over flowering plants and Pines; and, in what is by far the best mode, in houses especially erected for Vine culture, and hence named Vineries. It is also grown to some extent to fruit in pots, a system now much practised both for the decoration of the dinner-table and also for obtaining a crop of fruit while Vines planted out in the borders are coming on to bearing.

## SOIL.

Without the soil is right, all the other adjuncts, however perfect, will be useless. Whoever, then, intends to cultivate the Vine extensively and in perfection should procure, a year beforehand, a sufficient quantity of the top spit of the soil of an old meadow or pasture, choosing one which is neither light nor heavy, bringing away the turf and soil together, and laying it in a long ridge near to where it will be wanted. To every six loads of this maiden earth add one load of half-rotted stable-dung. Put this dung in thin layers amongst the soil throughout. To these add, in the same proportion, half a cartload of old lime rubbish, bits of bricks, and such like; also, a good sprinkling of broken bones—say a quarter of a cartload to the other seven and a-half loads of soil, dung, and bricklayers' rubbish. Lay the heaps so that the sun will have free access to every side, and in order to effect that the heap should run from east to west. Let the heap lie for three or four months, and then commence at one end and turn it over, thoroughly mixing the whole of the ingredients of the compost. Do not, however, chop it very fine, but leave it in lumps throughout, so that the air can penetrate into the centre of the heap as much as possible. As a matter of course, no weeds must be allowed to grow on the compost during the twelve months. Turn it over again in four months, and that turning will be sufficient till the Vine-border is ready to be formed.

Whether the Vines are grown in the open air on walls, or in houses, such a compost is the best that can be prepared for them.

But there are some soils in which the Vine succeeds very well without any preparation of the borders. These are loamy soils with a natural admixture of calcareous matter; those in limestone districts; or where the soil is largely composed of schistose and granitic detritus. In such soils all that is required is manure, and the Vine being a rather rich feeder this is not to be neglected.

## BORDERS.

DRAINING THE BORDER.—Whether the situation of the border be low or high, it must be drained. Stagnant water is injurious to the roots of any fruit tree, but more especially to the roots of the Vine. In low, level lands, the drainage should certainly be more perfect—that is, there should be a certain and sure outlet for the superfluous water, and the stratum of stones or brick ends should be thicker.

Let the bottom of the border be above the main drain, and sloping from the wall. It should be either concreted or rammed down very hard. The drain to carry off the water should be bricked at the sides, and covered with stoutish flags, so that in case of any stoppage from silt or tree roots it could be opened and cleaned out whenever required.

This drain having been made properly, and the bottom of the border made hard, then lay on the rubble of stones and brickbats evenly all over the border. In high dry lands this layer need not be more than 6 or 8 inches thick; but in low situations, even if the border of earth is raised above the level, the drainage ought to be at least 1 foot thick.

If the Vines are planted in a border inside the house, that border should be drained also. Level the drainage, and run a roller over it. Then, to prevent the finer parts of the soil falling into or being washed into the drainage, cover it over with thin turf, the grassy side downwards.

All this being completed, the next operation will be wheeling in the soil. Lay substantial planks to wheel on, and fill it up at the far end to the required thickness, and so on till it is completed. There has been considerable difference of opinion amongst writers as to the depth of the Vine border. Some recommend as much as 4 feet, others 3 feet, and some 2 feet. Deep borders are certainly very objectionable, because the deep stratum is often so cold and so far out of reach of sun-heat. However, to be on the safe side, we recommend that the border be 2½ feet deep.

# BORDERS.

The soil being all wheeled in, the border is then completed. It should at first be 6 inches above the level intended, to allow for settling.

The accompanying section (*fig.* 1) shows the

SECTION OF VINE-BORDER.

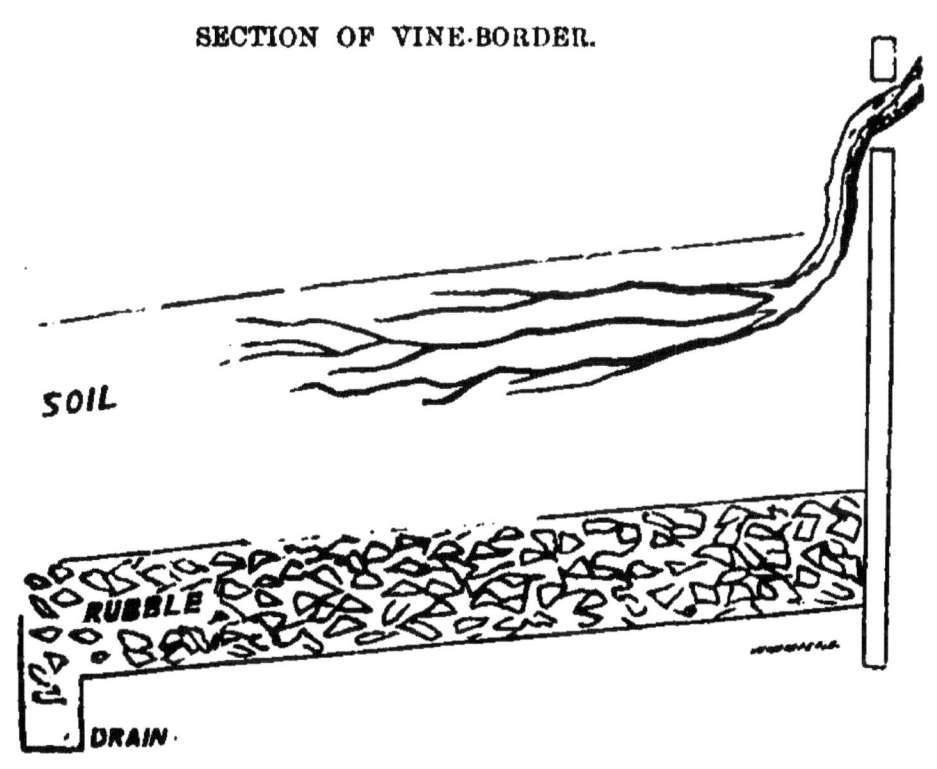

Fig. 1.

drain to carry off the water, the rubble to keep the soil dry, and the soil above it.

If planted outside a house, this mode may be adopted for admitting the stems of the Vines into the vinery without holes in the brickwork: a broad plate of thick wood projects about a foot from the wall, a semicircular piece is cut out of this for the Vine-stem to sink into, and the front lights can then shut down close upon the plate. In the annexed drawing (*fig.* 2), two windows are shown propped open, and one is closed. In some places a piece of wooden plate is fastened to each window, out of that the semicircular piece is cut, so that the plate shuts down upon the Vine-stem,

Fig. 2.

but causes all the front lights to project in a slanting direction, even when closed.

The practice followed by Mr. Henderson at Trentham was one of the best we have seen. We introduce the section of the house (*fig.* 3), chiefly to show the system of border-making, the border inside and outside being entirely above the ground level. The house is 11 feet in height from the path inside; the pathway is 4 feet wide; the front is about 2 feet above the sill, which rests on pillars, so as to give free egress to the roots out-

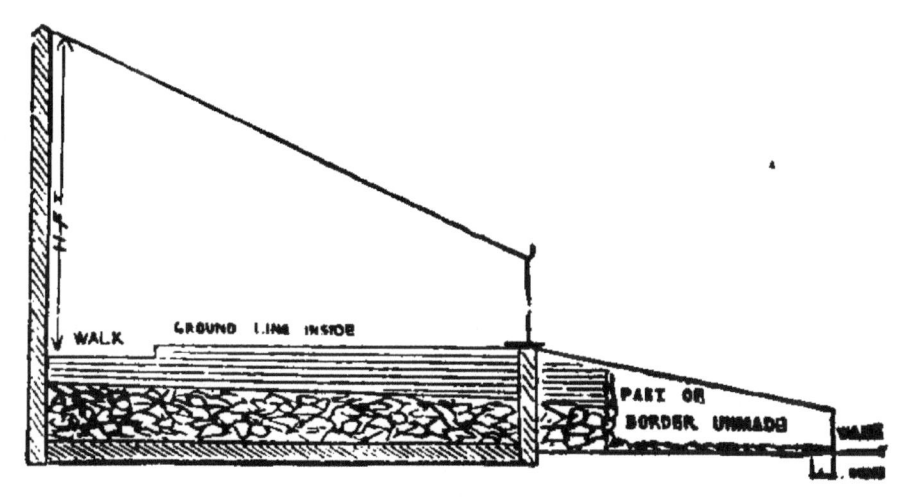

Fig. 8.

wards. The width from back to front is 16 feet. The outside border is 12 feet wide, and it will slope from the sill to the front, where it will be shallower. At the back, close to the sill, it will be 2½ feet deep, with 18 inches of large stones and rough rubble underneath. The soil was the best thin top-spit, with a fair allowance of boiled bones. Some of the bones that we examined were quite sweet, crumbly in the centre, and the roots passing through them. The outside of the bank of earth above the stones consisted of the roughest pieces of turf, and the air passing between the seams would render them very dry in hot weather. This very fact would have a tendency to send the roots back into the more moist soil behind. It was pleasing to find Mr. Henderson practising so largely, and not by any means in this house alone, the bit-by-bit system of border-making. This is done, not merely because part of a border can be more easily and conveniently made than a whole one, but because this bit-by-bit system contributes so much more to the continual luxuriance and fruitfulness of the Vines. When the roots have thoroughly permeated the yard width of the border, as shown in the section (*fig.* 3), then 2 or 3 feet more will be added in a similar way. Had the border been made to the front at once, the roots would have run along to the front, though there had been comparatively few lateral rootlets; and before these interlaced the whole border, much of the nourishing properties of the new material of the border would have been dissipated by decomposition and evaporation. Making a large border at once, and especially out of doors, seems somewhat analogous to the farmer turning a flock of sheep into a field of turnips, and allowing them to run and nibble where they may. The piece-by-piece border-making may be compared to folding the sheep, so that every available scrap of food shall be made use of, and a demonstrable compensatory influence be left behind them.

WIDTH OF THE BORDER.—For Vines growing against walls in the open air 10 feet or 12 feet will be sufficiently wide.

*For Vineries, Stoves and Greenhouses.*—The rule in general should be, that the border be the same width as the rafters are long.

In some Vine-borders brick walls are built, dividing it into as many sections as there are Vines in the houses. The reason assigned for this is, that each Vine could not encroach upon its neighbour's pasture; and also if by any chance a Vine failed, or it was thought desirable to plant some other kind, the soil could be all taken out of each division, and fresh put in without disturbing the Vines left to grow. This plan may be worthy of a trial, especially in conjunction with a heated chamber to warm the border of Vines for forcing early.

The borders should be made and finished as early in the autumn as possible, that the soil may be settled down to its proper level before planting time. Some authors recommend planting, after the Vines have made their spring shoots, in boxes, baskets, or pots; but the roots cannot be so well spread out in the soil without injuring some of the newly-made ones. We, therefore, prefer the planting just before the buds begin to swell: in that state the soil can be shaken out of the ball, and the roots disentangled without injury, and spread out in a proper manner in every direction.

## CHOICE OF PLANTS.

If the cultivator intends to purchase his young Vines from a nursery, he ought to go to the nursery early in the autumn, and choose the plants himself, marking them on the spot at once. Well-grown one-year-old plants raised from eyes are the very best for the purpose. If they are older the roots are so coiled round the sides of the pots that they cannot be uncoiled without some being broken, cracked, or bruised. Nurserymen now grow one-year-old Vines quite strong enough for planting permanently. The Vines should be sent to the purchaser as soon as their leaves are fallen—not later certainly than the end of October.

As soon as they arrive they should be unpacked carefully, so as not to crack any of the shoots. Let them be pruned to such a length as may be required. If they have to be brought through a hole in the front sill of the house, prune them so as to leave from four to five eyes within the house; but if they are to be planted inside, cut them down to three eyes. When all are pruned then plunge the pots either in leaves, old tan, or ashes, against a south wall, where they may remain till the planting season. If the Vines are intended for the open wall they may be planted out at once, protected with litter over the roots. By being pruned in autumn there is no danger of bleeding, which they are liable to do if pruned just before they are planted.

## VARIETIES OF GRAPES.

As a rule there is no better Black Grape for general purposes than BLACK HAMBURGH, and, wherever a general crop is required without regard being had to a number of varieties, we should recommend this in preference to every other. There is another form of this, called BLACK CHAMPION, the fruit of which is larger, more oval, colours earlier, and is ripe about a week or ten days earlier.

BLACK MUSCAT OF ALEXANDRIA, or, as it has been called of late years, Muscat Hamburgh, is, perhaps, the richest-flavoured of any Grape; but it is tender and a bad bearer on its own roots, and must, therefore, be grafted on the Black Hamburgh, when it succeeds to perfection, growing luxuriantly, and producing immense bunches of its jet black deliciously-flavoured fruit.

MILL HILL HAMBURGH is also a splendid Grape, having all the flavour of the old Black Hamburgh, but producing very much larger bunches, and immense round berries, like those of the Dutch Hamburgh, but much superior in flavour.

MADRESFIELD COURT is a remarkably handsome and fine Grape with large oval berries, and with a faint trace of the Frontignan flavour. It succeeds well in a cool house, and is as early as the Black Hamburgh.

TRENTHAM BLACK we would recommend for its delicious flavour. The flesh is very tender, and the skin is so thin that the berry, when fully ripe, is like a bag of syrup when eaten.

LADY DOWNE'S is by far the best of all the Black Grapes for late hanging. We have seen it in fine condition in the beginning and middle of April; and, where skilful management has been applied to it, there is no difficulty in keeping it till May.

WEST'S ST. PETER'S is also a fine late-hanging Grape, and, with this and the preceding, every purpose will be served without having recourse to a greater number of varieties.

GROS GUILLAUME has been highly extolled, but, in our opinion, it is not equal to many others.

GROS COLMAN is one of the very best of the late, or, rather, latest Grapes. Its enormous black berries, and bunches weighing from 3 to 4 lbs., form a handsome ornament in the dessert, and when well ripened in a high temperature its flavour is very excellent.

PURPLE CONSTANTIA is a sort somewhat resembling the Black Frontignan, but is preferable to it for its rich and peculiar flavour, which is superior to that of the Black Frontignan.

Among White Grapes there is none to equal, far less surpass, MUSCAT OF ALEXANDRIA. It has many names, such as Charlesworth Tokay, Muscat Escholata, and Tottenham Park Muscat. It requires more heat than Grapes usually do; and, therefore, if grown in a vinery of mixed sorts it should always occupy the warmest end of the house.

WHITE FRONTIGNAN, with the exception of Saumur Frontignan, is the earliest of the White Grapes having a Muscat flavour, and is a very richly flavoured fruit. It ripens with a much less degree of heat than Muscat of Alexandria, and may, therefore, be cultivated in a cool vinery.

DR. HOGG is the largest and finest of the White Frontignan class, the bunch being of large size and very handsome, and the flavour is very rich with a powerful Muscat aroma.

ROYAL MUSCADINE is the best of the early White Grapes not having a Muscat flavour, and is much relished for its fine refreshing flavour.

EARLY WHITE MALVASIA is earlier than the preceding, but the bunches are much smaller. It is, nevertheless, a finely flavoured Grape.

WHITE TOKAY, as a late-hanging White Grape, is one of the best. It produces large bunches and large oval berries exactly resembling Muscat of Alexandria, but without the Muscat flavour.

Calabrian Raisin is a superior late-keeping sort, and of good flavour, but it is not to be compared with the true White Tokay.

For an ordinary vinery containing—say, thirty Vines, we should select ten Black Hamburghs, four Muscat of Alexandria (to be planted at the warmest end of the house), three Black Muscat of Alexandria, one White Frontignan, two Dr. Hogg, one Grizzly Frontignan, two Purple Constantia, three Lady Downe's, one Madresfield Court, one White Tokay, and two Royal Muscadine.

## SELECTION OF VARIETIES.

For Walls in the Open Air.—Early White Malvasia, Saumur Frontignan, and Royal Muscadine.

For Cool Vineries.—Black Hamburgh, Purple Constantia, Madresfield Court, Saumur Frontignan, Early White Malvasia, and Royal Muscadine.

For Forcing.—Black Hamburgh, Royal Muscadine, Dr. Hogg, and Black Muscat of Alexandria.

For Stoves.—White Muscat of Alexandria, Lady Downe's, and Gros Colman.

## PLANTING.

The cultivator having procured his Vines, either from a nursery or by propagating them himself till they are fit to plant, the next operation will be the important one of planting.

For walls the best season is autumn; but the border, after the Vines are planted, should be covered with short litter to keep out the frost.

The planting of Vines in a greenhouse or stove should be deferred till March, but they ought to be planted before the buds begin to swell.

The mode of planting for outdoor culture will be somewhat different to that for indoor culture. The roots should be more spread out right and left, because each Vine will eventually cover more space; there will be, therefore, more space required for each Vine. In the sketch of the Vine-border at page 5, the roots are shown running across the border—the right plan, because each Vine only has the breadth of each light for its pasture; but on a wall in the open air each Vine trained, as we shall show presently, will have a space of 18 feet broad for its roots to ramble in: hence the roots should be spread laterally as shown by this sketch (*fig.* 4).

For planting choose a dry day, and turn out the ball entire, and pick out from among the roots all the soil. Then carefully uncoil and disentangle the roots, and remove a thin stratum of the soil sufficient in length and breadth to contain them. Then spread them out at equal distances, and cover them 2 inches thick with a compost of loam and leaf mould in a rather dry state. Some authors recommend decayed tan to cover the roots with; but that substance, when very rotten, has a soapy muddy appearance, and often in that state is poisonous to the young fibres.

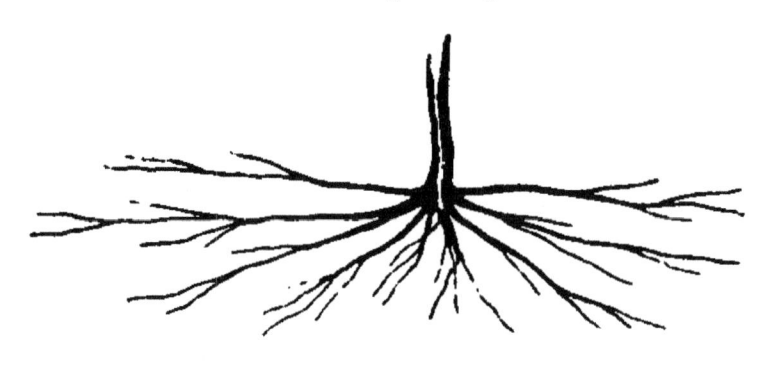

Fig. 4.

When all are planted, fork over such parts of the border as may have been soddened by treading upon, and cover the border with some warm stable dung, sufficient to give out a milkwarm temperature. To be quite perfect, the border, after the Vines are planted, should be protected from heavy rains, either with tarpauling or shutters just raised above the dung, resting upon a long piece of wood next the houses, and on a similar piece on the side of the border next the walk. Where the Vines are planted inside, this covering may be dispensed with the first year;

but when the roots have pushed through outside then this shelter ought to be applied as soon as the wood is ripe.

## PRUNING.

There are two systems of pruning applied to the Vine, the one called the "spur system," and the other the "long-rod system." We consider the former the better, because by it no strength of the Vine is lost, and, besides that, its simplicity, regularity, and neatness are great recommendations.

The spur system consists in cutting away, at the winter pruning, every side shoot from the main rod, down to one eye; and in the summer stopping these side shoots or laterals at the third or fourth joint, and, when the side eyes on the laterals burst, to stop these again and again throughout the growing season.

One very important point the cultivator of the Vine must attend to, especially where the spur system of pruning is followed, and that is to carefully preserve the leaf nearest to the bottom of the yearling shoot. That leaf has to mature the bud that is to yield fruit the following season. If it is destroyed, either accidentally or otherwise, it is probable that the shoot from that bud will not produce any fruit the following season: hence that leaf should be taken great care of till it falls off maturely ripe.

*Fig.* 5 represents how a Vine should be pruned on the spur system. In four or five years the spur may become long and unsightly, but at its base there is always a knot of incipient buds, one or more of which, when the Vine is vigorous, will break. Such a bud should be allowed to grow, and be encouraged to acquire strength by hard stopping the leading shoot on the spur. In the autumn, when the Vines are pruned, the old spur should be cut off, and the young one made to take its place. By careful attention the whole of the spurs may be renewed and brought, as it is called, nearer home. Mr. J. Meredith, of The Vineyard, Garston, near Liverpool, prunes his Vines still more severely. He cuts off all the spurs annually, and states that he very seldom fails to have fruit from the incipient buds; but then his Vines are so extraordinarily luxuriant and fruitful that he can afford to take liberties with them.

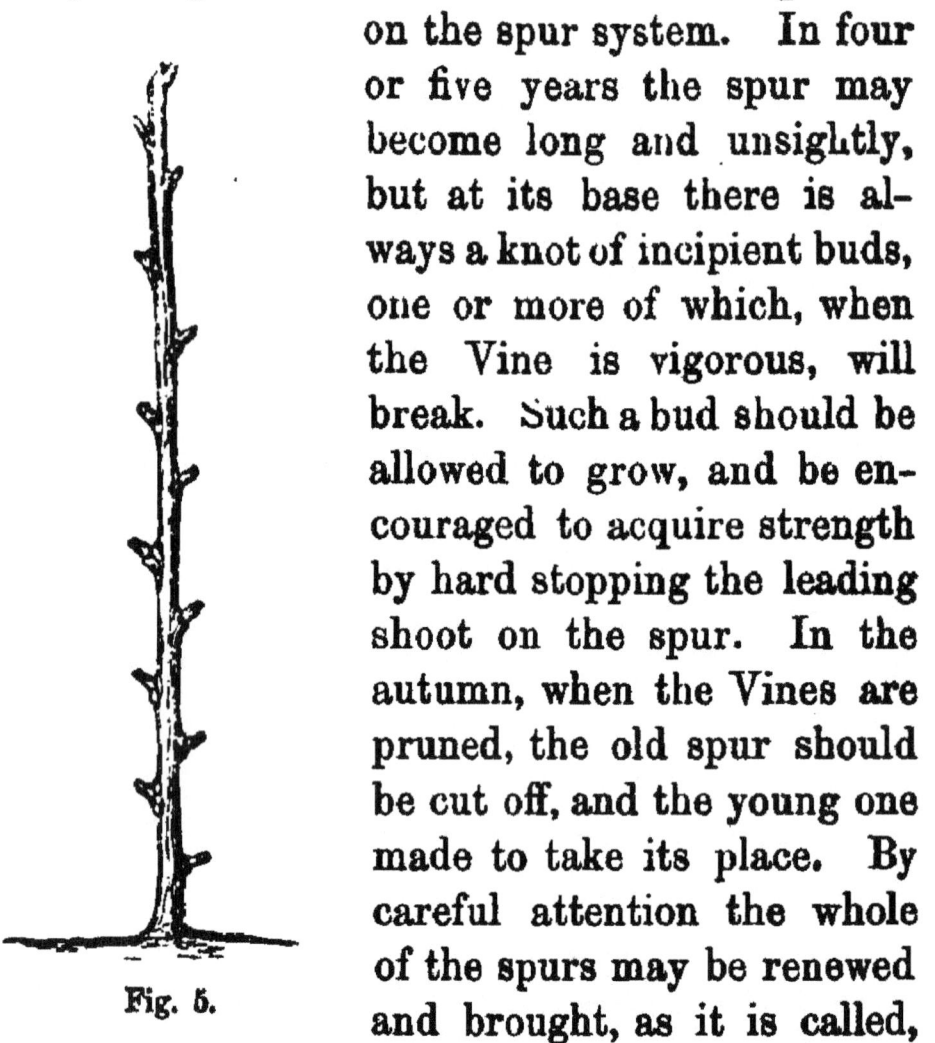

Fig. 5.

PRUNING.

The next best is that called the " long-rod system" (*fig.* 6). 1 shows a young Vine just planted and cut down to the bottom of the rafter at *a*, and one shoot only allowed to grow and to be

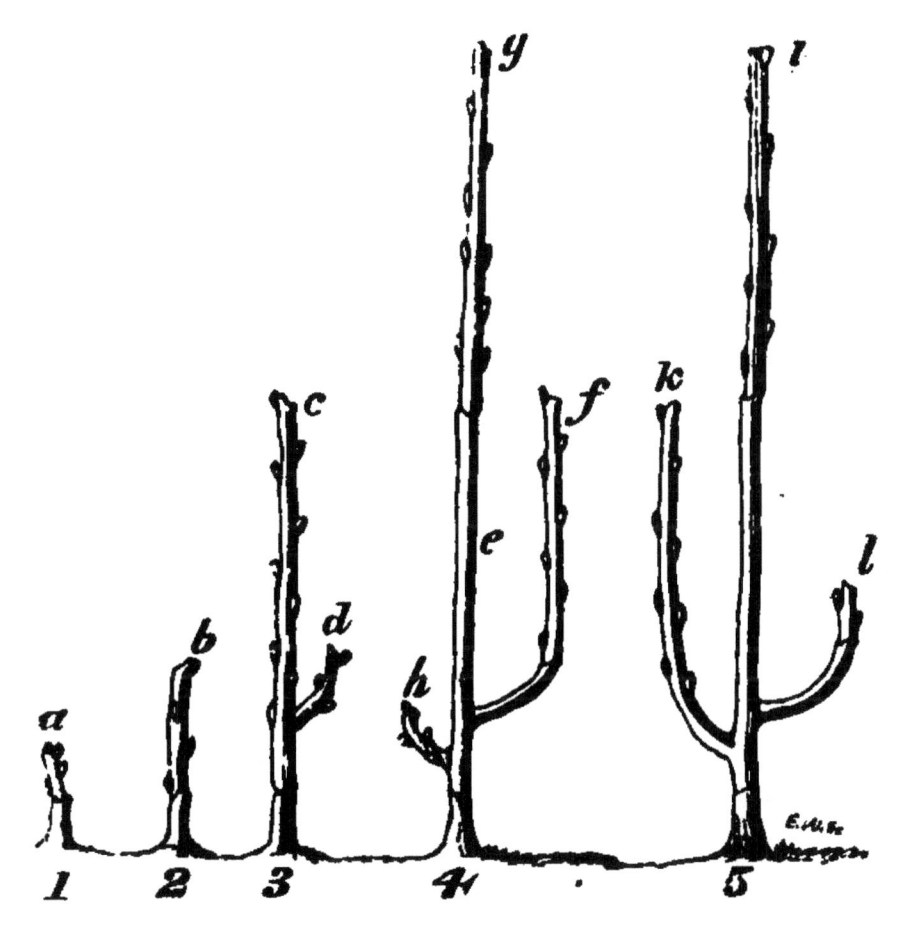

Fig. 6.

trained to the rafter. During that summer the Vine is allowed to grow if it will to the top of the rafter, and is then stopped. The laterals are also stopped at the first joint, and kept stopped from time to time as they break forth again. At the end of autumn when the leaves have all fallen and the plant is at rest, it is cut down to three or four eyes, as shown at 2, *b*.

The second year two shoots are left to grow, and the strongest is stopped when it has reached a foot or two beyond the middle of the rafter. The weaker is stopped also, but nearer to the place it started from. In the autumn following these two shoots are pruned as shown at 3, *c* and *d*. The leading and stronger shoot, *c*, is allowed that year to bear a crop of fruit, and the weaker one, *d*, is allowed to grow up by the side of *c*, and is stopped at a foot or so beyond it. The reader will perceive that the shoot *c* is bearing fruit that year, and the spur *d* is producing a shoot to bear fruit in its place the year after. The shoot from the top of *c* is allowed to run up to the top of the rafter, and is there stopped. The laterals on the upper part of *c* are stopped at the first joint, as also are those on the shoot *d*.

The winter following the Vine is pruned as shown in 4. The shoot made from the bearing-shoot *e* is cut off within a foot of the top of the rafter at *g*, and shoot *f* from the spur *d* is pruned to about the end of the shoot that has borne fruit. All the spurs on *e* are cut clean off close to the main stem. Each Vine, it is evident, now has fruit-bearing shoots that will furnish bunches from the bottom to the top of each rafter. The branch *f* may be trained close to the barren stem *e*, and the shoot that will spring from its top may be a little diverged outwards, so as not to interfere with the fruit-bearing shoot *g*. A spur at *h* is left to produce a young shoot the next summer to replace *f*.

In the autumn of that year the centre shoot *g* is cut out entirely, and the one *f* is brought into its place. 5 shows this—the Vine is pruned at *i*, which has reached the top of the roof, and at *k*, the shoot that grew from *h* (4); from *l* a young shoot will spring to supply the place of *f* (4). This completes the circle, and the same method must be followed year after year, always taking care that the rafters are furnished from the bottom with one shoot bearing fruit half way up, and another fruitful branch from the centre of the rafter to bear fruit to the top the same year, leaving a spur at the bottom to produce a shoot to replace the whole eventually. This system is very beautiful in practice, though tedious to describe. By it large bunches of excellent fruit may be produced.

## THINNING THE BUNCHES.

As a general rule, when two bunches are left on a shoot, neither is so good as when one only is left. We have satisfied ourselves that, taking weight and quality, the one bunch will beat the two. When, however, the crop is deficient, and there are two fine shows on a shoot, we should be tempted to leave them both, and in such circumstances we have had both swell well. If the crop is thin, the small ones on the other shoots might also be left; but if your crop is at all heavy, we

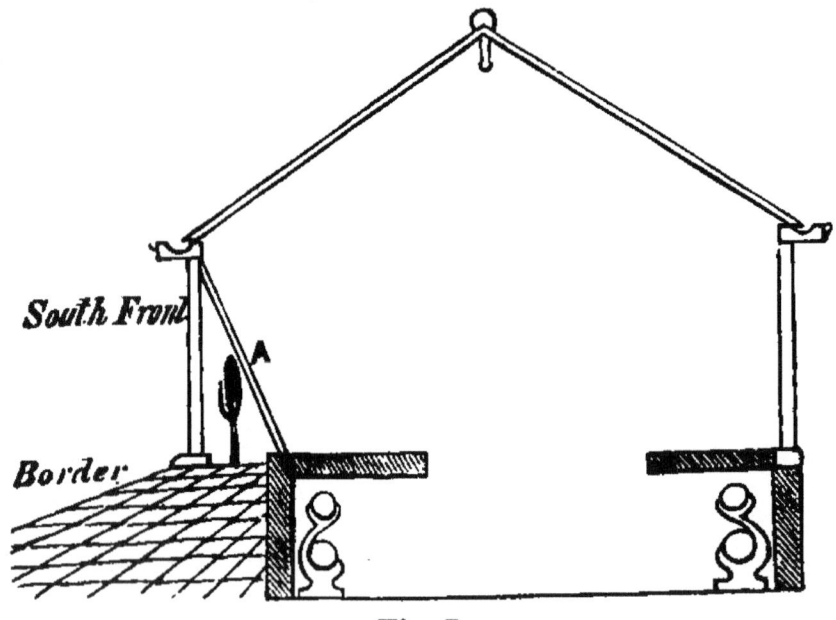

Fig. 7.

would certainly leave only one bunch to a shoot, even if you removed the small ones. We have frequently three or four bunches on a shoot; but, unless in the extreme case referred to, one bunch left was always most satisfactory in the end.

## RESTING VINES.

*Fig.* 7 represents a section of a small stove. It has a border at the south front, 18 inches of which are inside the house, and 10 feet outside.

There are five Vines planted in the border, and to get them to rest and still keep up the stove heat a temporary screen of glass, A, has been fixed.

By this not only are the Vines safe, and the house may be used for other purposes in winter, but the Vines may be kept back by giving air from the outside, and when they are to be started gradually a little heat can be allowed to reach them from the inside.

## LIFTING OR TRANSPLANTING VINES.

It sometimes happens that Vines, from a defective border, are subject to shanking, shrivelling, mildew, and other grievous calamities; and yet the Vines are neither too old, nor, as far as foliage and wood are concerned, unhealthy: hence it is thought to be a pity to cast them away— neither is there any necessity for so doing. They may be taken up and transplanted as safely as any other deciduous tree, provided due care is taken to perform the operation carefully, and at the right season of the year. The great object of lifting old Vines is to renew the border; and as that necessarily implies that the roots must be for a short time out of the soil, it is evident that the root-action will be totally suspended: hence the tree itself should be at rest also. This, of course, can only be the case when the leaves are all fallen. As soon as that has taken place the operation may be commenced—it is the right time. Yet Vines may be lifted and the border renewed even when the young wood is only partially ripened. It has been done, and successfully too; but it required such an amount of care in shading, syringing, and watering, that by far the best plan is to defer the work till both roots and branches are in a state of rest, especially when it is remembered that no balls of earth can be preserved to the long rambling roots of a Vine.

The cultivator, then, having determined to transplant his Vines, and at the same time to renew and improve the border, let him, some time previous to commencing the operation, procure and get ready all the necessary materials for the renewal of the border. These materials consist in a sufficient quantity of brick-ends, stones, &c., for drainage; next, a large heap of turfy soil taken from a pasture, mixed with about one-eighth of good hotbed or farmyard dung, about the same quantity of leaf mould, and a free proportion of rough lime rubbish, and also a good sprinkling of roughly-broken bones. Let all these materials for the soil of the border be thrown together and turned over frequently, to thoroughly incorporate the whole together. If the drains to carry off the superfluous water are defective, have bricks and tiles procured also in good time, so that no delay may take place when the Vines are in a proper state to be removed. That time having arrived, commence, with a sufficient number of hands, the operation. In order that the roots may not be out of the earth too long, let only three or four be lifted at once. Commence at the end, beginning at the side of the border furthest from the wall plate. Use three or five-tined forks only in removing the soil. Let it be wheeled away at once where it may be useful. Watch carefully for the roots, and as soon as the smallest are met with, carefully disentangle them from the soil, tying them up and putting them out of the way till the soil is removed. A few small stakes, or even pronged branches, the two prongs facing upwards, will be useful to preserve the roots; these supports can be removed forwards as the work proceeds. When that section of the border is all removed, and the roots safely preserved, have the bundles of roots wrapped in mats, and the mats occasionally sprinkled, to keep the roots moist and fresh. If this is neglected, and a drying wind or warm sun is allowed to act upon the roots, they soon dry up and shrivel, especially the best roots. The youngest, and consequently those that would stand, should start into growth first.

The old soil being removed, and the Vine roots

secured as much as possible from harm, then lose no time in first of all making the open drains perfect, and then wheeling in the rubble drainage. Of this useful and necessary material be liberal, especially if the situation is low and wet. That having been wheeled in, levelled, and rolled, then let it be covered with a thin layer of turf, the grassy side downwards; this will prevent the finer parts of the compost falling in amongst and choking up the drainage. That being completed, then begin to wheel in the compost, commencing close up to the walls of the house, and laying on a sufficient thickness at once; by so doing there will be no necessity for the barrow wheel, or even the feet of the men, ever to be put upon it—at least, until that part of the border now being operated upon is filled up again. One point must not be forgotten, and that is not to fill up the border to its full height—space must be left for the roots. It, however, must be remembered, also, that the soil will settle considerably; and therefore due allowance must be made for that settling. All these points having been attended to, then the border is ready for the roots of the Vines. Uncover them and spread them out regularly on the surface of the soil, treading on it as little as you possibly can. Finally, cover up the roots with the nicest part of your compost, about from 3 to 4 inches deep, and that finishes the operation so far as that number of Vines is concerned.

There the cultivator might rest for that year, and allow that portion of his vinery which he had removed to recover before lifting any more of his Vines; but if those unoperated upon are unfruitful, or produce indifferent Grapes, it would be better to have the whole renewed at once.

It is quite possible that some of the lifted Vines may not do well. Should that happen, then let young Vines be planted the season following, and let them gradually replace the old ones. Indeed, whenever a border is renewed, and the old Vines transplanted in it, young Vines should invariably be planted also the same season. If the old ones do well, it is easy enough to cut away the young ones; but if the lifted Vines do not promise to come round again, then a year is saved by having young Vines planted at once ready to take their place if necessary.

The after-management of lifted Vines is the same as for Vines that have no need of transplantation, with the exception that we recommend a severer pruning the first year: in some instances the Vines might be shortened-in considerably. This hard pruning would help to balance the loss of roots, and thus the roots retained, or rather preserved, would be able to send up nourishment enough for the reduced branches. Then, again, as the roots have all been brought up near to the surface, a greater care is needful to protect them from severe frost; and another point should be attended to, and that is, not to force them into action too early in the year—in fact, they will start more vigorously if not forced at all. Let the root-action be encouraged by warmth to commence first, and the top-action may be safely and better left to the natural heat of the spring sun.

## PROPAGATION.

Some gardeners raise their own Vines, and they are almost as easy to strike as a Willow. They may be propagated by layers, by lengths of two or three-year wood, by a small piece of two-year-old and two or three buds above, and by single eyes of the last year's growth.

Layering is, or ought to be, quite discarded; for when a layer is cut off from the parent stool it receives such a check that it requires two or three years (even with the best management) before it recovers the separation.

Cuttings.—Old shoots also require considerable care to make them push roots sufficient to support a strong young shoot. The two-year-old wood, cut off a few inches below the point where the young wood of the same year has pushed from, makes good cuttings, and with little care makes good plants the following year. We have grown good Vines by this plan, fit to plant out the following year. The only objection is, that a stump always remains at the base of the Vine, which is liable to decay sooner on that account. Raising Vines from cuttings, however, is now rarely practised, for they root too slowly in the open ground to allow of the young shoots ripening; and, even if promoted by bottom heat, the young growth subsequently increases so much faster than the whole wood of the cutting, as always to be unsightly, and frequently to cause ultimate failure. If cuttings are used, select at the autumn pruning the well-ripened, medium-sized, short-jointed shoots; cut them into lengths of six buds each, and make the cuts so that an inch of wood remains beyond the terminal buds. Insert one end of these cuttings into common garden soil, in a pot, and keep it in a cool situation, but free from frost, until March; from the middle of which month, until the end of the first week in April, is the best time for planting them. Plant them in a sheltered situation, such as at the base of a west wall, and let the soil be mixed with a little sand or cocoa-nut fibre dust, before planting them. Mulch the surface about them during summer. Each cutting should have two buds; one to be inserted about 2 inches below the surface, and each bud should have an inch of wood beyond it. Plant them immediately after being thus prepared, pressing the earth firmly about them. The young shoots should be fastened to the wall to prevent their being broken off by the wind.

Single Eyes.—These approach the nearest to seedlings, and for permanency form the very best plants. In saving wood for buds to raise young Vines avoid coarse strong shoots; choose rather such as are round and of a medium strength, with as little pith as possible, and also choose the cuttings from Vines that have been forced early—not only because the wood is sure to be well ripened, but also the buds, in the natural course of the season, will be more easily excited to start early. Also prefer the buds that are nearest to the preceding year's wood, taking care, however, that each bud is plump and sound. Take off the shoots intended to be propagated from as soon as convenient, label each bundle correctly, and lay them in by the heels in a shady border.

Towards the middle of December place some soil, composed of fresh good loam, leaf mould, and very rotten dung, in equal parts, in a warm shed to dry. Have ready a sufficient number of pots $3\frac{1}{2}$ inches wide. Then, about New Year's-day, bring the cuttings inside, and cut them into short lengths, one bud to each length. An inch in length will be sufficient. The part behind the bud is then reduced in thickness, and cut off in a slanting direction towards the ends, and the part under the bud horizontal. The cuttings will then have this appearance (*fig.* 8)—

Fig. 8.

Fill the pots nearly up to the brim, and with a small dibble insert one bud or eye in each pot quite overhead. To prevent mistakes, do all one kind first, and place a label or number to that lot before commencing with the next variety. This method of putting the eyes at the first in separate pots is much better than placing a number in a shallow pan or wide-mouthed pot, because in repotting not a single root need be injured. When all are potted and securely labelled, then place the roots in a propagating house, on a platform covered with sand. Under the platform there should be hot-water pipes, and there should be a sufficient extent of pipes to get up a heat of 70°. At first, however, a temperature of 50° will be sufficient, and raise it 5° every week till the maximum is reached.

During all this time a moist atmosphere should be kept up in order to cause the eyes to swell and break kindly. In a month or six weeks every bud will be breaking through the soil and forming roots. Keep the soil regularly moist, but not wet, for too much water would cause some to damp off. As the leaves begin to expand more water may be given.

Examine a pot or two occasionally by turning out the ball carefully, and as soon as the roots reach the sides of the pots generally, then place a lot more of the compost in a warm place to air it. Cold soil at this stage would chill the young roots and check their growth. As soon as it is sufficiently aired, then begin to repot the young Vines, being always careful to keep them from draughts of cold air.

Shift them into 6-inch pots, giving plenty of drainage. These pots will carry them on growing till the middle of May, when a second repotting may be given them, placing them in 8-inch or 9-inch pots. They will now require more room and plenty of air, and liberal supplies of water and liquid manure. Place a tall stick to each Vine, and look sharply after red spiders and destroy them. After a sunny day use the syringe freely, which will keep down insects and encourage growth.

In these pots such as are intended for planting

out may be allowed to finish their growth. They should make shoots in them 8 feet or 10 feet long, and as thick as a penholder.

If it is desired to fruit a few in pots, then give such another repotting in June, into 14-inch pots, using more loam in the compost, to give solidity to the wood. Vines for this purpose should be stopped when 10 feet long, and should have more light and space to each.

By starting the eyes into growth as early as described above, the cultivator will have the advantage of getting his Vines into strong growth early, and thus be enabled to obtain good plants with well-ripened wood before the summer is over.

GRAFTING.—The border of a vinery may have been properly drained, heated, and made of the best soils, the Vines planted and growing healthily and satisfactorily, and yet some kinds that have been planted may either not be true to name, or newer and better kinds may be desirable. The owner, in order to save time, may graft the superior sorts upon these healthy Vines. Procure the scions, choosing well-ripened, short-jointed wood, a year old, some time before the season arrives, and plant their lower ends in sand, in a shady place, and have ready some grafting-wax or clay.

The *grafting-wax* is made of Burgundy pitch 1 lb.,

mutton fat 2 drachms, yellow wax 2 ozs., black pitch 4 ozs., and rosin 2 ozs.; melt the whole together in an earthen pipkin or other vessel gently over a slow fire, stirring the mixture constantly till all is thoroughly mixed. Whilst hot, pour it into a glazed pot or tin, and keep it slightly stirred till it cools; it is then fit for use.

*Grafting-clay* is formed of some very strong loam, of a clayey character, adding a little water and beating it with a mallet, and kneading it with the hands until it is soft and putty-like, and of a uniform consistence. Then obtain some horsedung, dry it slightly, and then rub it through a half-inch meshed sieve. Take some cowdung, just dropped, and mix the three together in equal parts; knead them thoroughly, and add a little finely-chopped hay, also sifted; this prevents the clay cracking. Then put through a very five sieve some dry ashes, and keep these dry in an open vessel. When the clay is applied to the graft the hands should be dipped in the ashes, and that will enable the workman to finish off the ball neatly and close around the graft. It is immaterial whether the wax or the clay is used.

The right season for grafting the Vine is just when the buds of the stock to be grafted are beginning to swell, the scions being kept at rest till that time arrives. Vegetation in the stock should always be in advance of that in the scion.

## PROPAGATION.

The best mode is the common one, named whip or tongue-grafting. The engraving (*fig.* 9) illustrates this mode—*a*, the scion; *b*, the stock. Choose a well-situated branch or lateral near the bottom of the Vine; cut the head off slanting at a part where a scion can be fitted on best; then cut a slice off upwards about 1½ inch long, slanting inwards; make an incision downwards about the centre of the last-made cut, taking great care that the knife does not slip through nor yet injure the bark on each side; then prepare the scion. The scion should have one bud near the top, and another near the bottom; make a sloping cut downwards as near the same length as that on the stock as possible, and in or near the centre of this make an upward cut, which forms the tongue; lay the knife down, and gently thrust the tongue into the cut on the stock. Every part of this operation must be done with a knife as sharp as a razor, and every part should fit neatly and perfectly. One point must be particularly attended to, and that is, that the bark of the scion and the bark of the stock meet

Fig. 9.

exactly together on each side if possible; but if the scion is smaller than the stock, then the barks must meet on one side and at the bottom. This being successfully accomplished, tie with matting the scion pretty firmly to the stock, and then cover the whole of the cut parts with either the grafting-wax or the grafting-clay, excepting the uppermost bud of the scion. If a little moss is tied gently round the clay-ball, it will keep it moist and preserve it from cracking. If the scion pushes freely, and when it has made a few leaves, it will be necessary to remove the wax or clay, and untie the matting, and tie it again more loosely, to allow the parts to swell in the natural way. By thus grafting on a lateral, the main stem of the Vine may bear its crop of fruit; but, in order to strengthen the shoot the scion is making, all the other shoots on the main stem should be kept closely shortened, and no more wood and leaves allowed to grow than are necessary to bring the crop of fruit to perfection: hence, if any shoots are barren, let them be pruned away entirely. In the autumn the main stem should be cut away down to the graft, and the fresh kind trained up in its place; or, if the scion has not grown strong, the lower half of the laterals may be pruned off, and the upper half left on to bear a few bunches the succeeding year, previously to removing the main stem.

Another mode of grafting the Vine is one that has been practised very successfully. When the plant is in leaf, head down the stem to the point where it is to be grafted, and split the crown, inserting the scion, cut into a wedge shape, on one side of the split, taking care that the barks of the scion and the stock fit exactly (*fig.* 10). Bind it round with a piece of matting, and cover with damp moss or clay. If the stock is very thick, two scions may be inserted, one on each side of the split.

INARCHING.—This is a kind of grafting very suitable for the Vine, and also very safe; for if it is properly done, and at the right season, it cannot fail. As in the case of grafting already described, the stock should be healthy both at the top and at the root. Some writers recommend strong-growing varieties, such as the Syrian and White Nice, to be planted purposely to be grafted or inarched with weaker-growing sorts, such as the Frontignan, thinking thereby to improve and strengthen them. To graft upon unhealthy Vines, thinking to

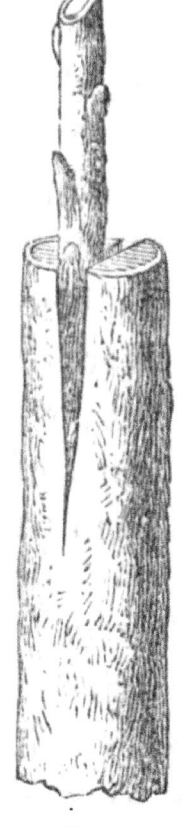

Fig. 10.

obtain good Grapes from such grafts, is simply ridiculous.

Inarching is grafting by approach—that is, a branch or stem of one kind is brought into contact and joined to a branch or stem of another, each kind growing on its own roots at the time.

Procure the new or superior kinds in pots, and, as in the case of grafting with scions, let the stock be a little advanced in growth, and the one to inarch upon it not so forward. Place the pot securely, near enough to the stock, in a convenient position to form a junction with it. Place the shoot of the one in the pot close to the stock, and then pare off, with a sharp knife, a slice from each of equal size; bring the two wounds together as exactly as possible, fitting bark to bark; hold them firmly in that position, and tie them together firmly, but not so tightly as to bruise the bark of either. Then tie a little moss round the junction, and moisten it every day with the syringe. Should the sun shine strongly upon that particular point, it will be desirable and useful to shade it for a week or two. The sap in action on the growing stock will soon flow into the branch united to it, and will cause the buds above the junction to push quickly and vigorously. Keep the soil in the pot moist, and rub off two or three buds below the junction. One or two near the bottom may be allowed to grow to draw up the sap; and thus, when the part above is firmly united to the stock, the pot Vine may be cut off at the junction, and made use of, either to be planted out, or grown to bear fruit in a larger pot.

Inarching on young wood of the present year's growth is often practised—indeed, preferred by many; but it requires greater care, for the young wood is tender, and, consequently, more liable to be broken than year-old wood. Choose, as before, a young shoot near the bottom of the main stem, one that has grown some length should be preferred, and inarch upon it when it has acquired some solid wood, just when it is beginning to change colour. The plant in the pot should also have grown some length, and have been placed in a position so as to be convenient for inarching, fixing the pot securely, so that it will not slip away; bring the two shoots together, and take a slice from each of an equal size; then fit them closely and tie securely, but not so tightly as in year-old wood. This young wood unites even more quickly than older wood, and the junction will be complete in about a month or six weeks. Whilst it is growing let all the bearing-shoots be kept closely stopped, and any that are barren should be pruned off closely. Afterwards treat the Vine and its successor the same as is directed for those inarched on year-old wood. By either of those methods a vinery filled with inferior kinds may be renewed with superior and newer kinds in a much shorter time than by grubbing the old Vines up, and replanting with year-old Vines.

RAISING NEW KINDS.—The only way to raise new kinds is by seed, and in order to multiply the chances of obtaining improved varieties it is advisable to cross them. Large-berried Grapes are often mere water and sugar, yet large berries are desirable: hence, in order to throw a superior flavour into their progeny, the pollen from some highly-flavoured variety should be employed as the fertiliser; and, to make more sure, cut off all the anthers just before the pollen-vessels burst, and then dust the stigmas with the pollen from the full-flavoured variety.

Save the seed from well-ripened fruit, and let it be sown immediately it is taken from the berry. Sow in pans, in a rich sandy soil, and either plunge the pans in a brisk bottom heat, or place them on a hotbed in which Cucumbers are growing or intended to be grown. The seedlings will soon appear, and then they should be potted off in small pots, to be repotted every six weeks—in fact, treated just the same as plants raised from eyes. Train the young shoots upwards, without stopping for that year. In the autumn following cut them down to two buds, and train up one shoot from each. If well managed, some will bear fruit the third year, and all, certainly, the fourth. Superior kinds may have a fair trial; but tasteless wild growers may be at once thrown to the rubbish-heap.

## VINERIES AND BORDERS.

There is no doubt that the management of the Vine is the most successful and most certain in houses built expressly for the purpose. To grow it to the greatest perfection, and to furnish good fruit all the year round, three houses are necessary, one for the earliest crop, another for the summer crop, and the third for the autumn and winter crop. In large establishments this division is still further carried out, by having houses planted with some kinds that require peculiar treatment—as, for instance, one house is filled entirely with the Muscat of Alexandria Grape, or allied kinds, because such sorts require a higher and drier temperature when ripening than others; and then, again, another house is planted entirely with the West's St. Peter's Grape, and similar sorts, to ripen in the darker months of the year. The best form for a vinery is the span-roof, provided it is properly ventilated at the apex, to let out the superabundant heat that accumulates there. If the house is intended to be forced early, then have the border entirely inside; but for a general crop, in order to give the Vines a large pasture, let the walls be built on arches, and have additional borders on both sides. The aspect of such a vinery should be east and west. It will then have the benefit of sunlight from the morning to the evening. These borders would be improved and made more perfect if chambered and heated as described before. In other respects, as to the compost, draining, and sheltering, we have nothing to add to our former details.

For the early vinery the border should be entirely inside, because then the root-action goes on simultaneously with the top-action—a very important point; for the sap cannot flow freely from roots in a cold soil, exposed to all the severity of winter. It, however, must be borne in mind that a border covered with glass has no chance of receiving moisture from rains: hence water must be supplied freely, so that the soil may be wet quite through. Just at the time when the fruit is swelling, two or three waterings with liquid manure may be applied with advantage, more especially after the borders have been occupied with the Vines for three or four years. Manure water for this purpose may be made as follows:—Have large tubs kept for the purpose. Procure the dung from the poultry-yard and pigeon-cote, and, if that be not sufficient, add to it a quantity of cowdung, collected clear of straw,

To this add a lot of soot and a small quantity of quicklime. With these manures fill the tubs about a third-part full, and then fill up with hot water, stirring the whole well together right down to the bottom of the tub. As soon as it cools down to a milkwarm temperature, and the heavier particles have settled down to the bottom, apply it to the borders when they are moderately dry. If it is judged to be too strong, then that strength can be reduced by adding tepid water sufficient for the purpose. The lime and the soot effectually kill any insects that may be in the dung, and the hot water destroys their eggs. Should there be any worms in the border or pots, this kind of compound liquid manure kills them also. The borders inside the summer and autumn vineries should, in the growing season, have a supply of water sufficient to thoroughly moisten the soil.

As the fruit and wood ripen the watering should be more moderate, and be finally relinquished when maturity is accomplished. Then every part of the vineries should be kept as dry as possible, both to prevent the Grapes from moulding and the leaves from decaying prematurely.

COVERING OUTSIDE BORDER.—We do not think that any Vine-border wants covering or thatching from June to August. For pretty early forcing it would need covering from the second week or the first week in October, to the end of May or the beginning of June. To cover so early as August would be to deprive the border of the hottest rays of the sun for the season; and covering should only be resorted to when the doing so will keep the border warmer and more regular in temperature than when exposed.

Slates alone we would disapprove of, because in severe frost the ground would freeze beneath them. Wooden shutters, half an inch thick, and strengthened by cross and end bars, would be better and quite as light to move; but in frosty weather, and in early forcing, we should like some litter or fern beneath them. This litter can only be dispensed with in such circumstances as when the roots get so deep as not to be affected by sudden changes in the weather. Shutters would be liable to the objection of occupying room after they were removed from the border; but they could be put close together without injuring each other, and, when not wanted for the border, might be made of sizes to suit covering pits and frames, and other purposes. We have seen such shutters or covers made 6 feet by 4, with cross-bars, and a ledge all round 1½ inch deep, costing about 6s. each, that have been in use more than a dozen years and hardly ever idle, and they seem not a whit the worse. Strong tarpaulin may also be obtained at about 1s. per yard; and if a little fern or litter were placed on the border, and some rough slabs or poles over that, to keep the tarpaulin stretched and free from the litter and the ground, it will last many years, and be easily put on and taken off and stowed away. Such tar- aulin is very useful for throwing off heavy rains in autumn, even when you wish the atmosphere to have free access to the border. Altogether, however, when economy more than appearance is to be considered, placing litter on the border and rough-thatching it would be best. The disadvantages are chiefly that in heavy snows it is difficult to get it off without injuring the thatching, and that the border consequently is apt to be soaked and cooled. To guard so far against this, we will mention two plans that have been pretty successfully adopted. In both cases the surface of the border is made smooth. This secured, Mr. Judd, at Althorp, had a heap of lime, sand, and very fine gravel, which he watered, and mixed, and put on the border about 2 inches thick or so, beaten or rolled smooth, and the litter put over it. Scarcely a drop of rain will go through it. In May or June, when the litter is removed, this concreting is also removed, placed in a heap, and, with a little fresh lime and sand, and fresh mixing, it lasts year after year.

This is the plan that used to be followed in the case of the early houses; and, by a pipe placed longitudinally along the border, and a few inches from the surface, and a thermometer thrust down by the pipe by means of a long rod, the temperature could always be seen and noted. The other plan has been frequently adopted by Mr. Fish. After smoothing the border, a few barrowloads of fresh cowdung, if procurable, were plastered thinly over it, and on that as thin a layer of coal tar as could be drawn with the spade or trowel. generally thinner than a sixpence. No water will go through that. Over the tar is thrown a sprinkling of sand drift, or sawdust, and then, when deemed necessary, a little litter is thrown over to keep out frost, and is generally increased as the forcing commences. In May or June, when the litter is removed, the thin coating of tar is easily removed with a sharp spade or shovel. If a strong sun beats on it for a few days it will often lift in good large pieces. Such tar being generally procured at about one penny a gallon, a shilling's worth will do a fair-sized border for a fair-sized house. In putting it on the man should use a plank to stand on, so as to make no footmarks. It spreads more quickly and easily if the barrel or vessel containing it is put into a fermenting dungheap, so as to heat it a little. The workman should have something tied round his legs, to prevent any drops falling on his trousers. He may roll up his shirt sleeves, and not mind a few spatters on his hands or arms. Candle grease, soap, and hot water will remove all traces almost as soon as any other dirt. The rubbing the places with grease before applying the soap and water is important.

On the whole, then, unless the roots are deeper than we like them to be, we would use less or more litter on the outside border of forced Vines. For covering that border we would prefer wood covers or shutters, or waterproof canvas, free of the litter; and next to these we would prefer litter and rough-thatching, with or without the above means of surfacing the border for the winter.

HEATING.—Very good Grapes may be, and indeed are, grown where the heat is furnished by common flues; but there is always danger of flues bursting by internal explosions of confined air, or other cause: hence it is now allowed that there is no system of heating so safe and easy to manage as that of circulating hot water in iron pipes connected with a sufficiently large boiler and fireplace. Let us, in this place, warn against false economy in those two important points— namely, the size of the boiler and the extent of piping. There can hardly be too much of the latter, for it is easy to manage the fire so as to heat the water moderately; but it is not so easy to heat a large body of air to the right temperature, if the boiler is small and the pipes deficient either in size or number. Three or four pipes will give out more heat from a given quantity of fuel than one or two filled with water nearly to boiling heat, besides being much safer and easier to manage; therefore have plenty of piping, and a boiler large enough to heat the water moderately.

Another mistake in regard to the situation of the pipes is placing them close, or nearly close, to the soil of the border. Though heat ascends, it also radiates, and that radiated downwards dries up and parches the soil of which the border is made. That is an evil which may be easily avoided by placing the pipes upon stands a foot or more, as may be convenient, from the ground. By so arranging the hot-water pipes, the drying of the soil will be prevented.

The vineries that are devoted entirely to the Muscat of Alexandria, Canon Hall, and allied kinds, require to be kept very dry when ripe or nearly so, in order to produce that high, rich amber colour for which they are so justly admired: hence there should not be a single plant allowed in them, for the necessary watering of plants sends up a moisture that is injurious to these Grapes. The best plan is either to cover the entire internal floor with flags; or, if that is inconvenient, let the floor, by which we not only mean the walks but the borders also, be covered with clean dry gravel.

HEATING THE BORDER.—All are agreed that it is advantageous to have the temperature of the soil where the roots of the plants are growing, approximating somewhat to that in which the shoots are, especially in cold damp climates, and in early forcing. We know that in the pot-culture of plants, generally speaking, they succeed best when the roots are in advance of the stem, or in a medium where the shoots can be supplied from the root with the food suitable for the perfecting of the whole plant: if this be correct, which experience leads us to think is the case, it follows that the general treatment of the Vine hitherto has not been that which it ought to be; this would appear true, from the different modes that have been adopted to increase the temperature of the soil. The natural habit of the Vine and our own reason lead us to conclude that it is seldom treated as it ought to be. True, good Grapes have been, and will be, grown without any artificial heat to the soil; but this is no reason why those same Vines might not have been better, had the temperature of the soil been higher than it was.

Having to erect new vineries at Yester, the annexed drawing (*fig.* 11) is the plan Mr. Shearer adopted—it being the desire of the Marquis of Tweedale to heat the soil by some means or other, he being led to do so from his observations on the

Fig. 11.

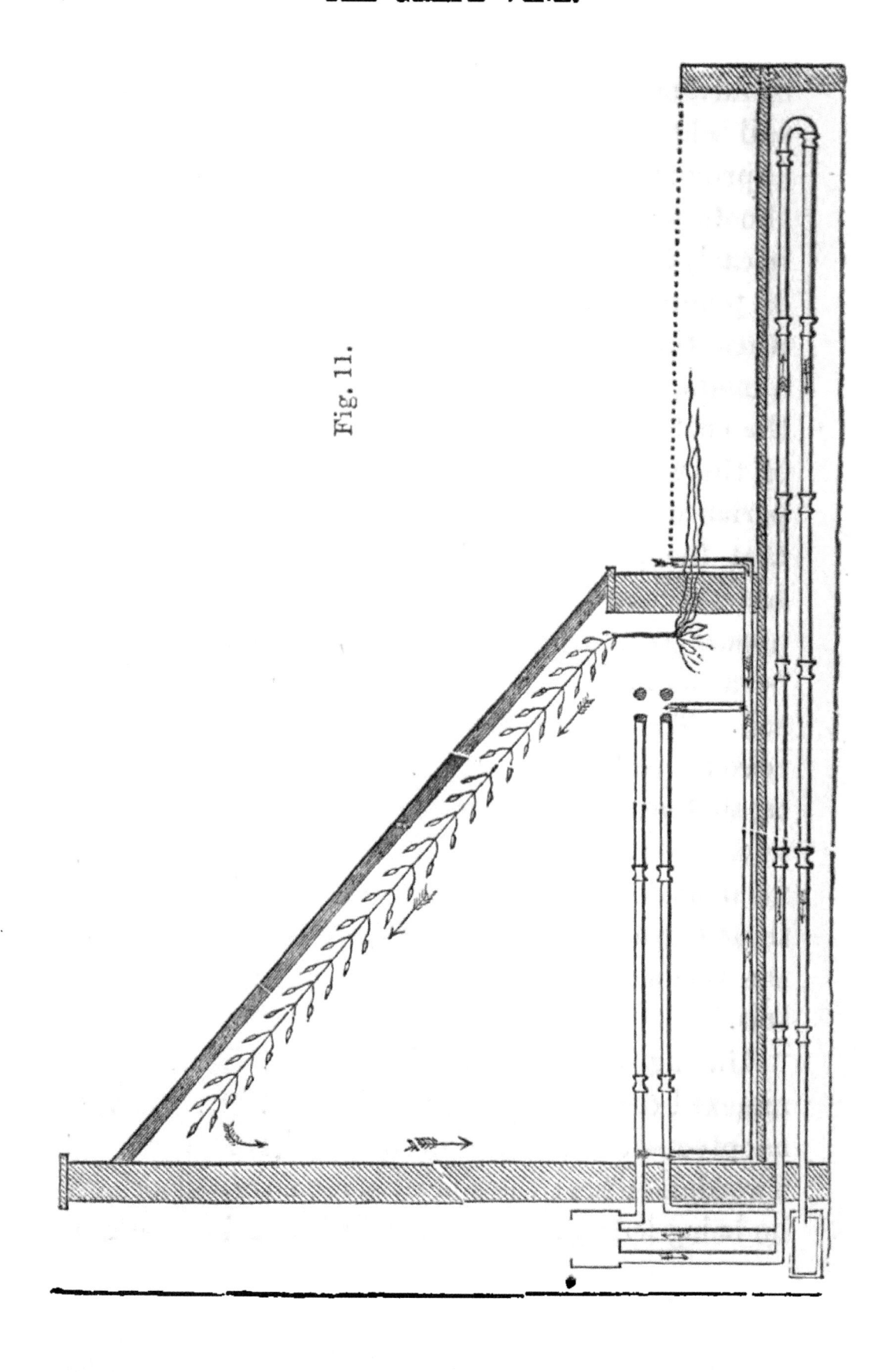

temperature of the soil when in India. To do so by means of hot dung thrown under brick arches was objectionable, from the amount of labour required to keep up anything like a steady heat. To cover the surface with dung was still more objectionable, from its unsightliness, its bad effects on the border, and its being opposed to the well-known laws of the conduction and radiation of caloric.

"We were led to adopt the Caithness pavement, which is 2 inches thick, and in pieces from 3 to 4 feet square; also moderately cheap. With this was constructed a chamber, 2 feet 6 inches high, with 9-inch brick pillars supporting the pavement, and heated with hot-water pipes from the same boiler which heats the houses. We have found it to exceed our most sanguine expectations. In the first place, we have a thorough drainage, and the roots cannot by any means get into the bad soil below; but the most important fact is, that the temperature of the soil in the chamber at 2 feet deep is at all times 9°. higher than that of a border of the same aspect not chambered. When the frost has penetrated into the latter 9 inches, it has only reached 2 inches in the chambered border—that is, without any artificial heat being applied. The increase of 9°. was quite unlooked for when the border was chambered; but being supplied with soil-thermometers, for the purpose of ascertaining the temperature of the soil in various parts in the garden, and in the farm, throughout the year, we had an opportunity of knowing the fact; while, under other circumstances, it might not have been known. It also led his lordship to cause to be chambered upwards of 300 square yards of wall-borders, for growing early vegetables, which, when made, indicated the same increase of temperature as the soil—viz., 9°.

"The question will naturally arise, Can the temperature of the soil be raised to any great extent by the hot-water pipes, with a single mat covering the border, to prevent radiation in any sort of weather, excepting rain? We can raise the temperature of the soil from 50°, up to 80° in eight or ten days, with a very small amount of fuel, much smaller than we could have imagined. By this mode of heating we could keep the soil where the roots are at a temperature of 80°, while the shoots would be at the freezing point, by merely opening or shutting the valves of the hot-water pipes."

In order to find out correctly what effect a quantity of fermenting dung, laid on the surface of a Vine-border not chambered would produce in raising the temperature of the soil at 1 foot 6 inches deep, on the 17th December, 1849, Mr. Shearer covered the border 3 feet deep with good fermenting stable-dung and leaves, turning it occasionally, and adding to it. When the dung was put on, the temperature of the soil was 40°; on the 17th January, 1850, it was 42°; 17th February, 53°; 17th March, 53°; 17th April, 53°; 17th May, 58°. Until the end of March the temperature of the dung was from 70° to 90°, when it fell gradually until the end of May, when it was taken off. On the 17th of June, by the heat of the sun, it had risen to 60°; July 17th, 63°. While that quantity of dung raised the temperature of the soil 13°, the chambered border stood till the 17th of February (when the hot water was let on), at 49°, only 4° lower than the unchambered border with all the dung. From this it would appear that the dung has little effect in heating the soil. It only prevents radiation; and a slight covering has nearly the same effect as a greater thickness of fermenting dung.

LEAN-TO VINERIES.—For these we will select as a good example those at Keele Hall, where Mr. Hill has performed such astonishing results in Grape-growing. Each house is 31 feet long, 16 feet wide, 10¼ feet in height at back, and 3 feet in height at front. These heights refer to that above the surface level. The front, 3 feet above the wall-plate, is of glass sashes, opening outwards all at once by a rod, &c. The border inside is nearly up to the glass A (*fig.* 12). B is the back path, 4 feet wide, bounded by a neat curb, from which a pillar (c) goes to the roof at every 4½ feet. On these pillars, in some instances, Vines are also trained, and an arch goes from pillar to pillar. The borders are chambered or arched underneath. The outside borders (E) are 9 feet wide, and are arched underneath at F, communicating with linings (G), covered with board flaps, so that dung may be placed under the arches and the heat kept

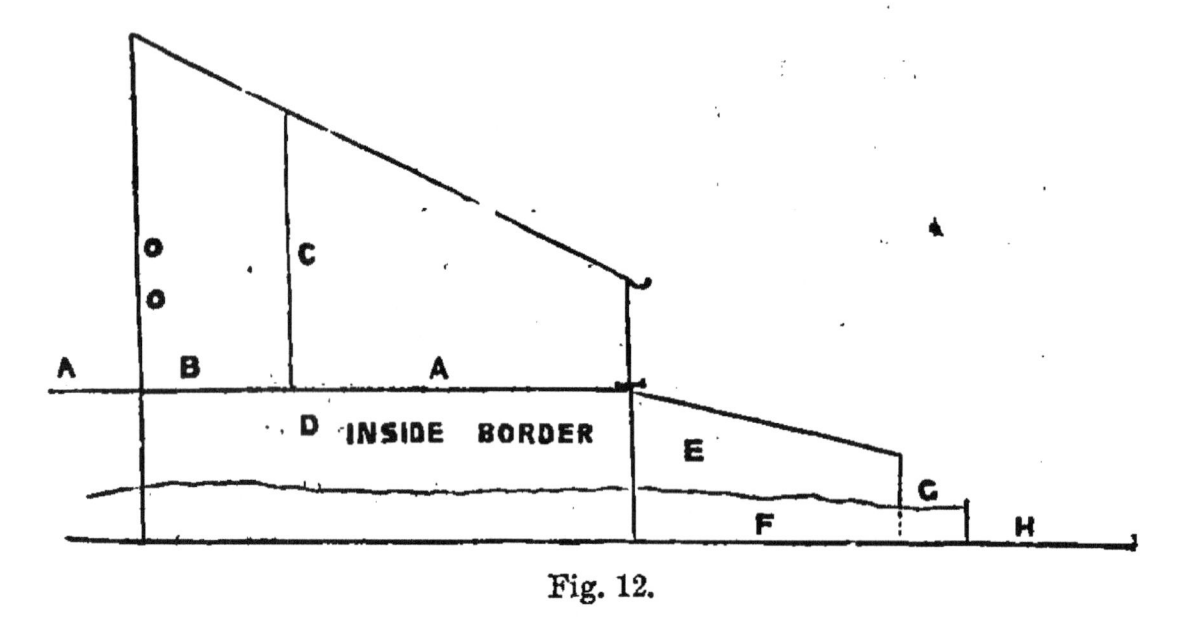

Fig. 12.

in. H is the pathway in the front, and the ground gently falls from the pathway.

The elevation of the borders, the chambering, and means used for drainage, render it impossible that the Vines can suffer from stagnant moisture, and therefore nourishment can be freely given to them. The Vines are all planted inside, about 18 inches from the front glass, and in every case the inside border is higher than the outside one, but with free communication between them. All the heating pipes are 4 inches in diameter, and are placed pretty regularly and level across the floor of the house—a plan which we consider far preferable to placing pipes in tiers above pipes. There is an exception to this placing the pipes on the level, and we consider a valuable one, in the shape of two small 2-inch pipes, placed over each other some 18 inches from the base of the back wall. These, so placed behind the pathway, prevent any stagnation of air there, make the circulation of the internal atmosphere more complete, and alike enable and require top ventilation to be more freely given. Then, instead of sinking a pit for a Vine-border, it will be perceived that the whole, inside and out, is above the ground level; and then, again, there is the opportunity of heating these borders from beneath. The arches are formed of brick and good mortar, so that little or none of the enriching gases from the dung can reach the roots, nor is it desired they should do so. A root now and then may find its way through the mortar into the chamber, but it is soon destroyed by the heat, or removed. This mode of heating the borders from beneath with dung involves a great amount of labour and constant supervision, as the heating material is subject from mere changes of

56     THE GRAPE VINE.

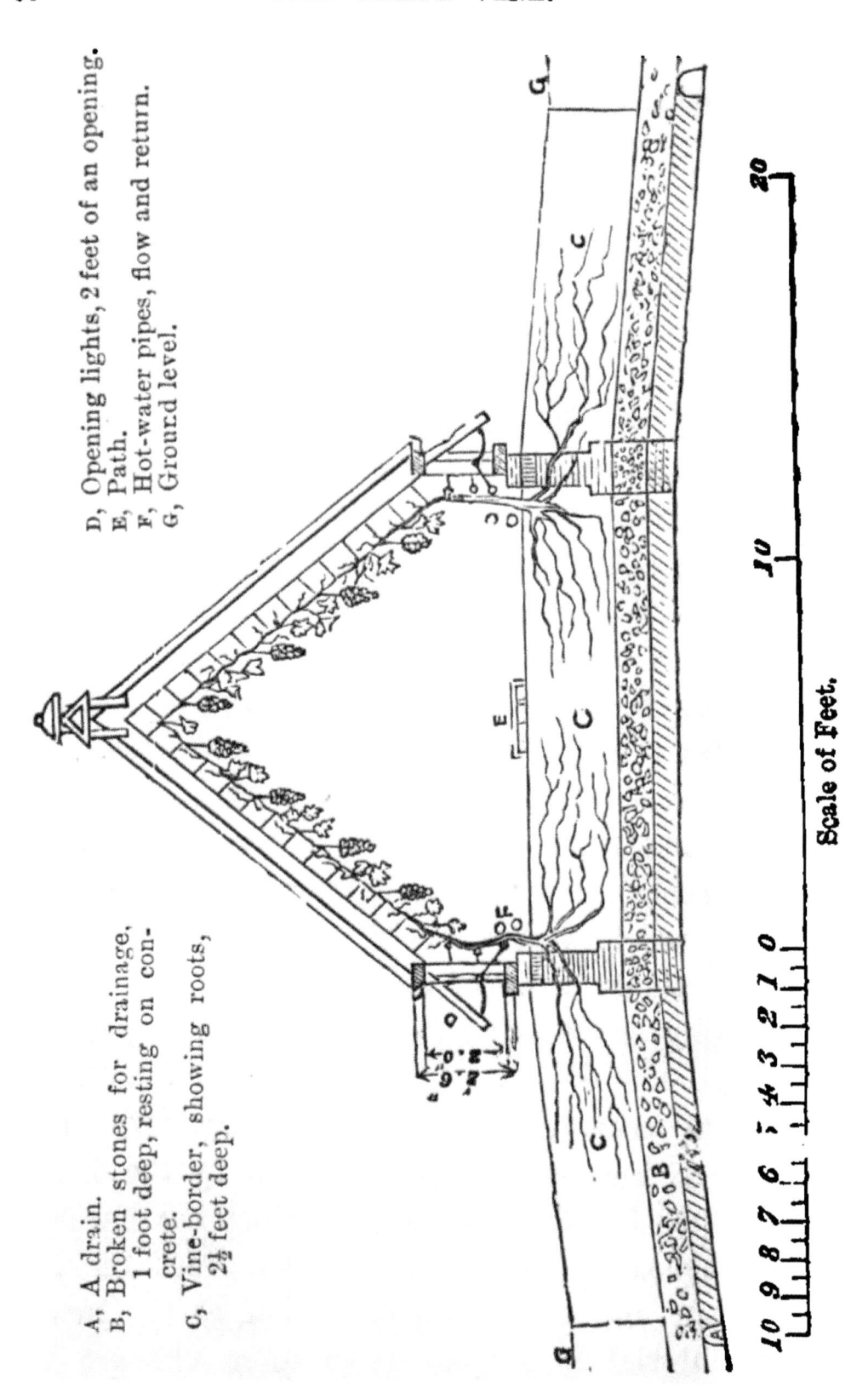

A, A drain.
B, Broken stones for drainage, 1 foot deep, resting on concrete.
C, Vine-border, showing roots, 2½ feet deep.
D, Opening lights, 2 feet of an opening.
E, Path.
F, Hot-water pipes, flow and return.
G, Ground level.

Scale of Feet.

Fig. 13.

# VINERIES AND BORDERS.

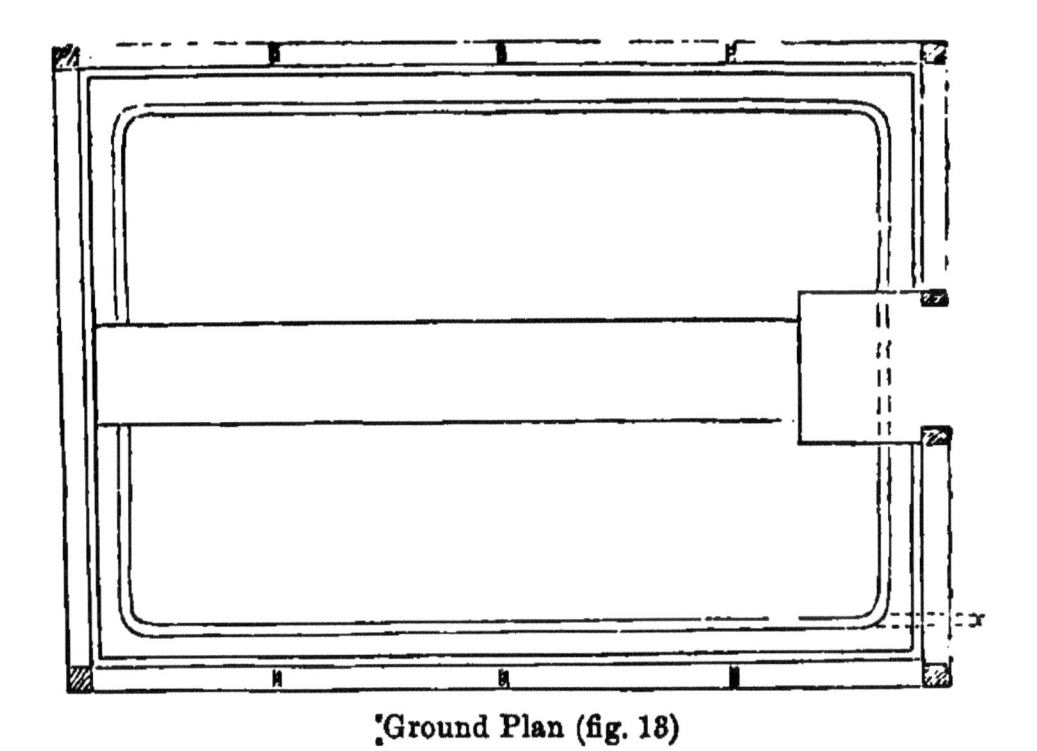

Ground Plan (fig. 18)

Side Elevation, showing the openings for roots (fig. 13).

weather to great and sudden fluctuations of temperature.

On this account it is proposed to dispense with the dung, and use hot water, as being much more under command. With this heating from beneath, a slight covering—say from 9 inches to a foot—of dry leaves or litter is sufficient to keep up the desirable temperature in the borders, more especially as that covering is kept dry by moveable wooden covers 4 feet wide, and in lengths so that one or two lengths go over the border. These covers are made of rough boards fastened to cross pieces, and then a slip 2 inches wide tacked along each joint—a capital plan where green unseasoned wood is used, and even for any wood exposed to great alternations of wet and dryness. These, well tarred, will last a great many years, and will come in for many purposes of protection in the spring and autumn.

SPAN-ROOFED VINERIES.—The accompanying plan (*fig.* 13), represents a span-roofed vinery, the dimensions of which will be found suitable for the generality of amateur growers. Its length admits of six Vines at a little more than 3 feet apart, which space is not by any means more than is necessary to do Vines anything like justice as to room. The span-roofed is what we regard as the best form for vineries in all cases, except that of very early forcing, when a lean-to facing direct south is preferable. The span-roofed house running north and south gets the sun early in the morning and late in the afternoon, while at all periods there is a greater diffusion of light, and Vines under such circumstances always make finer foliage and wood, and, as a consequence, bear finer Grapes than in a lean-to, which loses the morning and evening sun enjoyed by the span-roofed structure.

The house, of which a plan is given, to bring it quickly into full bearing, should have six Vines planted on each side, and afterwards, should there be any desire for such, one of the sets may be trained down the other side.

The lowest part of the surface of the border is shown at the same level as that of the ground, but in damp localities and in heavy cold subsoils it is well to keep it at least a foot higher, which, of course, necessitates the brickwork being higher; and cross drains should run from the centre of the house to the main drains A.

The side ventilation is effected by a rod and quadrant, and the capping on the top is raised in much the same manner for top ventilation.

For Muscats it will be well to have three rows of pipes along each side instead of two, as shown in the plan.

The wires to which the Vines are trained should not be nearer the glass than 16 inches.

## THE GRAPE VINE.

VINERY AND PEACH-HOUSE COMBINED.—This plan is very successfully carried out by Mr. Stevens, gardener at Malvern Hall, Solihull, and he thus describes his procedure:—

"I forward you a sectional view (*fig.* 14), of what I consider our most productive house. It is

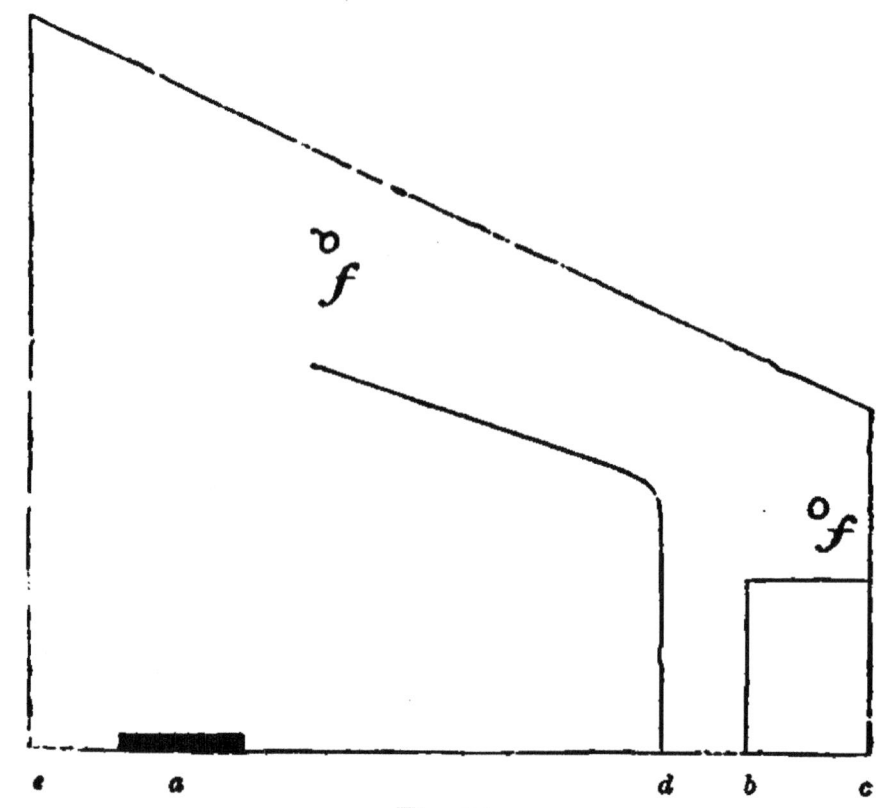

Fig. 14.

*a* Principal path through the house.
*b* Front path parallel with *a*.
*c* Front flue.
*d* Wire trellis, with one Elruge and one Pitmaston Nectarine.
*e* Back wall and wire trellis, with one Royal George, one Noblesse Peach, and one Elruge Nectarine.
*f* Black Hamburgh Vine suspended from rafters.

an old-fashioned lean-to, 30 feet long and 13 feet wide, height at back 12 feet, ditto front 5 feet, and it is heated by a flue running round the house, the return flue being built in the back wall. The front wall is on arches, which allow the roots of either Peaches or Vines to ramble at will.

"The Vine is planted in an outside front border. It is furnished with spurs its whole length, and has not failed to produce from eighty to ninety bunches of good Grapes every season since I undertook its management nine years ago. The house also produces fine Peaches and Nectarines. The front and ends of the flue are covered with a stage, which is useful for storing Strawberries in pots during winter; and this being what we call our second Peach-house, we get a crop of Strawberries in it a month or six weeks before the out-door crops are ready.

"After Strawberries, Capsicums in pots take their place, as we can do but little with them in the open air in this cold district.

"The bed under the front row of Nectarines I find is a capital place for Dwarf Kidney Beans in pots. On this bed last year I had several Red Currant trees potted in No. 3-sized pots the previous autumn for the purpose. They were only three-year-old trees, and I trained the young shoots down balloon-fashion. They not only looked pretty, but they each produced enough fruit for two good-sized tarts, and were six weeks earlier than those in the open garden."

## VINES IN THE STOVE.

Grapes may be grown exceedingly well in conjunction with Pine Apples and what are generally termed stove plants. In such houses the heat is generally high, and, consequently, those Grapes requiring more than ordinary heat may with advantage be cultivated — such as Muscat of Alexandria, Canon Hall Muscat, Dr. Hogg, Charlesworth Tokay, Mrs. Pearson, and Bowood Muscat. These are light-coloured Grapes. In dark-coloured, Muscat Hamburgh, Black Hamburgh, Lombardy, Mrs. Pince Black Muscat, Lady Downe's, and Gros Guillaume. The White, Red, and Black Frontignans are excellent Grapes, and where the stove or stoves are large, would be an acquisition. West's St. Peter's is a good late kind, but is more suitable for a vinery. In places where there is no vinery especially devoted for an early crop, it would be desirable to plant a few Vines that would ripen earlier than the above kinds, and such are Royal Muscadine and Chasselas Musqué. By this arrangement Grapes may be had in the stove from June to the end of the year. The late kinds, Gros Guillaume and Lady Downe's, would keep the latest.

There are two points in the culture of the Vine in a stove that are somewhat difficult to overcome. The first is the application of heat to the roots so as to obtain root-action simultaneously with top progress; and the other the necessary rest after the fruit and wood are ripened. By a little skilful management both these difficulties may be successfully obviated.

Supposing that the stove to grow Pines or plants has to be put up, and expense is no object, then contrive the building so that there shall be a narrow border inside between the hot-water pipes and the outer wall. This outer wall to be so built that there shall be arched openings opposite every Vine; and, to make sure, let the outer border itself be placed upon an open chamber, that chamber to be filled with air warmed with hot-water pipes, with shallow open troughs fixed on them. At the time of commencing to force the Vines these pipes should be gently heated, and the troughs filled with water; the chamber under the roots would then be filled with a moist agreeable temperature, which would excite the roots into growth simultaneously with the buds; and, to make doubly sure, the open border should be protected from frost, snow, and heavy rains by a waterproof covering of either boards or oiled canvas nailed to frames. This sort of shelter is much superior and neater than a heap of littery dung or even dried leaves; for these materials soon become cold and wet, and, consequently, ungenial, if not injurious to the roots. The accompanying section (*fig.* 15), will explain the mode much more plainly than mere description.

The water on the pipes inside the heated chamber might be easily supplied by a small lead pipe connected with them from the inside of the house, and pierced with a hole opposite each

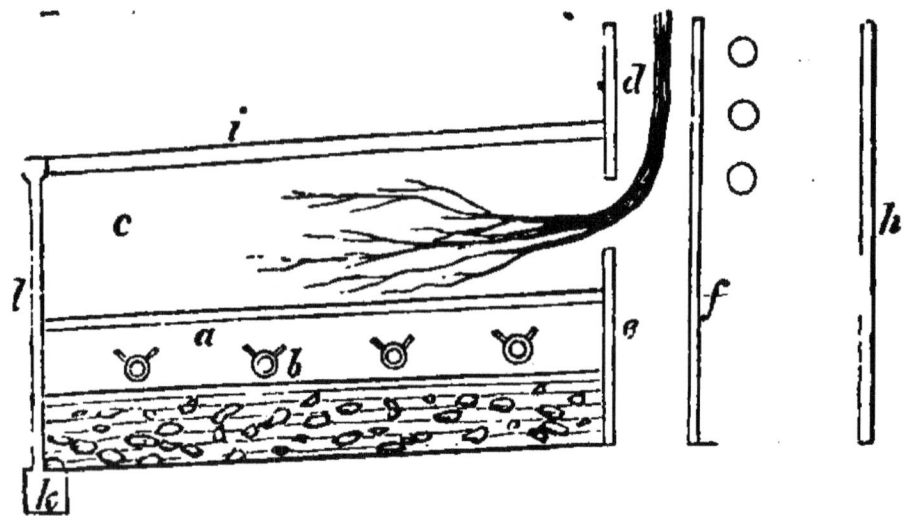

Fig. 15.

Section No. 1 of Vine-border, with border inside and a heated chamber under the border outside.

*a* Heated chamber.
*b* Pipes in the same with troughs on them.
*c* Outer border.
*d* Inner border.
*e* Front wall.
*f* Inside wall of inside border.
*g* Walk, and pipes to heat the house.
*h* Wall of pit for Pines or plants.
*i* Shelter for border outside.
*k* Main drain.
*l* Drain to carry off the water from the covering.

trough. Section No. 2 (*fig.* 16), explains this part.

It is evident when all these parts are in working order the air inside the chamber will be warm and moist, and as heat rises the border above will be gently heated also. The roof of the chamber should be formed with flags resting on bricks, and the pipes might be conveniently placed between each row of bricks. The hot-water pipes in the chamber can be supplied and heated by being

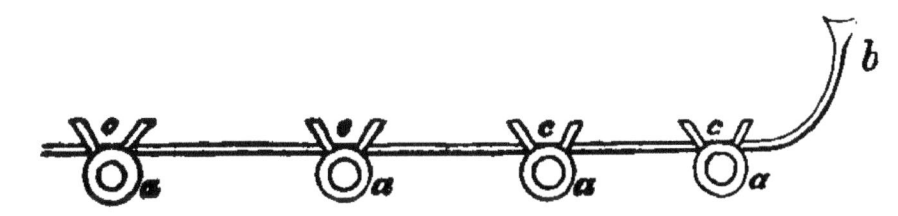

Fig. 16.
Section No. 2, showing the mode of filling the troughs in the heated chamber under the Vine-border of a stove.

*a a a a* Large Pipes.
    *b* Small lead pipe with a hole drilled opposite each trough.
*c c c c* Troughs.

connected with the boiler that heats the pipes inside the house.

The second difficulty—namely, the giving the Vines the proper rest, and at the same time keeping up a proper temperature for Pines and stove plants, is more easily overcome than inducing root-action early in the spring. There are two ways of accomplishing this: the best is the having a double front—that is, a range of glazed frames set upright on the front wall (*e*, section 1, *fig.* 15), and a second range of glazed frames to rest upon the inner wall (*f*, section 1, *fig.* 15). Now, when the Vines are growing the inner range is taken away, and may be made useful for other purposes

F

during the summer. After the fruit is all gathered and the wood thoroughly ripened, then the Vines should be taken down from the rafters, pruned, and laid down close to the outer range of frames, and when completed the inner range should be fixed up and made air-tight. The Vines are then, as it were, in a long box, which may be kept as cool as you like by opening the front lights every day and night, and also in mild weather. The house, of course, will be heated as usual for its permanent occupants.

The second mode is managed thus: The front lights are made moveable, and when the Vines are pruned, they are laid down close to the glass as in the first manner; but then the lights are removed and brought inside, set up on the inner wall, and made air-tight by placing a shelf on the top of them, that shelf being so broad as to reach to the bottom of the roof lights. This plan answers very well, but not quite so well as the first. On the shelf any low-growing plants may be placed, thus giving more room to the rest, such as dwarf Lycopodiums, Achimenes, and Gloxinias, when at rest, and many other similar things that require a medium heat.

PLANTING.—The best time to plant Vines in a stove is when the temperature of that house is the lowest, which takes place generally in winter: therefore we recommend the planting to be done any time in February, the earlier part of the month being the best. The object is to secure a gradual starting into growth. There is nothing gained by over-forcing young Vines as soon as they are planted; indeed, if the double-front system is adopted at first, the young Vines might be planted as early as New Year's-day, and the roots gradually induced to grow whilst the shoots are kept cool. The same method of spreading out the roots in a fan-like fashion should be adopted as much as possible.

PRUNING.—On this head we need only say that the best mode is the spur system, which is described in another chapter.

SUMMER TREATMENT.—This consists in the usual stopping of laterals, setting the shy sorts, such as Canon Hall Muscat, Black Morocco, and Muscats of sorts, with the pollen of more free-setting sorts. The Black Hamburgh, for instance, has abundance of pollen, and as it is a free bearer there are generally a few bunches to spare for this purpose. The flowers of these shy setters should be examined previously to applying the pollen, and care taken that the lids that cover the stigmas are fallen; for if they are still adherent, applying the pollen will be useless. A little care at the proper time on this point will almost be certain to cause plenty of berries to set, even on the shyest kinds.

## VINES IN A GREENHOUSE.

The kinds best adapted for a greenhouse are Black Hamburgh, Madresfield Court, Royal Muscadine, Grizzly Frontignan, White Frontignan, and Prolific Sweetwater. More kinds might be tried, but the above are good croppers and sure to answer.

PLANTING.—The best season is March, just before the buds break.

PRUNING.—The best mode of pruning for a greenhouse is undoubtedly the spur system; and for this reason, that the foliage is less in quantity, and, therefore, does not shade so much the plants that are in the house than when the single-rod system is adopted.

*Summer Pruning* consists in stopping the laterals at the third or fourth joint, and, when the side eyes burst, to stop these again and again throughout the growing season. Every fruit-bearing shoot should be stopped at the second joint above the bunch. When the fruit begins to colour, the first-made laterals should be cut off close to the stem, in order to give more light to the leaves and fruit.

*Autumn Pruning.*—The Vines in autumn may be half-pruned by cutting off all the laterals, in order to ripen the wood and fill the buds with fruit-bearing sap. As the leaves turn yellow they should be removed.

*Winter Pruning.*—This may be done in any of the winter months after the fruit is all gathered and the leaves have all fallen. At that season the greenhouse plants will all be housed. It is more convenient to prune the Vines by loosening them from the rafters in succession, bringing each one down into the walk or path, commencing at one end, pruning each side shoot to one eye as directed before, and, when that Vine is pruned, clearing away the loose bark and applying a paint made of water thickened with sulphur and clay. Use a softish brush, and see that every part is covered with the sulphur. This mixture is a great preventive, if not a cure, of mildew, and destroys scale and red spider. Then tie the Vines down to the front in a bundle. In that position they may remain till the buds begin to break. By being thus trained horizontally at the lowest part and consequently the coolest part of the house, every bud will be in an equal temperature, and receive an equal amount of sap; hence the lower part of the rafter will be as well furnished with fruit as the higher, and the berries will swell almost equally as fine as those on the higher part of the house.

A former race of gardeners recommended that Vines grown under glass should be fully exposed to the severity of winter by removing the windows or other mode. No good gardener adopts such treatment now. No advantage is ever so obtained, whilst there is much liability of injury to the Vines, and a great endurance of labour and inconvenience.

SPRING MANAGEMENT.—The Vines may be allowed to remain in this horizontal position till the laterals can be stopped, but when this is done you must be very careful of the young shoots, for in their young state they are easily slipped off at the base. There is, however, a great convenience in doing this work when the Vines are so handy and easily examined. As soon as one Vine is operated upon—that is, the superfluous shoots rubbed off, the fruit-bearing spurs stopped, and, if long enough, tied slightly to the main stem—that Vine may be tied up to its proper rafter, and the next taken in hand, and the same operations gone through till every Vine is done. It requires at least two persons to do this: one to hold the Vine, and the other (the more experienced hand, of course) to thin out the shoots and stop those that are left. In lofty greenhouses crowded with plants, this spring dressing, when the Vines are tied up to the rafters before it is done, is a very difficult and troublesome affair.

SUMMER MANAGEMENT.—This consists in regularly stopping the laterals and keeping them tied in neatly to the wires. There should be three wires—one in the centre to tie the main stem to, and one on each side of it to tie the laterals to. Each wire should be about 9 inches from the glass, and 6 inches from wire to wire. To keep them in position there should be strong iron pins, sharp at one end, or made with a screw, and an eye at the other end; the wires run through those eyes, and they keep the wires in their proper place. If the wire is pretty strong, the pins will do if placed 6 feet apart. Thus trained, when the Vines are in full bearing all their length, the bunches hang in two straight rows, and are very ornamental. The laterals should not be trained at right angles, but rather slanting upwards. If the Vines are very fruitful, never allow more than one bunch to a shoot. The spurs should be as nearly as possible a foot apart, and at equal distances. When the Vines are in bloom the air of the house should be moderately dry. In general, the air should be more moist during the night than during the day. Alternate moisture and dryness will cause the anther-coverings to contract and expand, and eventually to crack and open when the pollen is ripe and ready to be shed upon the stigma. If all this has gone on properly, the berries will set freely and will soon begin to swell. Then is the time to commence thinning them—an operation that must not be neglected. Thin freely, and you will have larger berries, but handle the berries that are left as little as possible. Most of the kinds proper for a greenhouse have bunches with large shoulders. The bunch will be more symmetrical, and each berry will ripen more equally if those shoulders are tied up and spread out equally on each side. Some use pronged sticks for this purpose, but soft matting is the better article, and the branches of the bunch can be by this mode spread out more equally. While the thinning is going on examine the laterals and ties, and top the one and adjust the other.

SYRINGING.—During summer, before the Grapes begin to colour, give them a good syringing once or twice a-week, especially after a hot sunny day.

WATERING.—This will be required at the root in dry weather; manure water of any kind and quality they will greedily devour. This, if not more successful, is more refined to men's general feelings than filling a border for Vines with rank garbage, such as the carcases of animals. As to watering overhead, we recommend the disuse of the syringe and engine as soon as the buds are fairly broken. Moisture in the atmosphere may sufficiently be maintained by watering the stages and floor of the house. If that great pest, the red spider, makes his appearance, he should be dislodged by lighting a fire in a dull night, and painting the flues and pipes with a solution of water and flowers of sulphur. If in a flue, be careful that you put none of the sulphur near to where the flue enters, as it ignites at a comparatively low temperature, and then will kill everything green in the vegetable way.

Air, of course, will be given very freely in the early stages of growth, because of the plants; but as soon as the greenhouse plants are removed out of doors, towards the end of May or beginning of June, less air will do for the Vines. The stage of the greenhouse will then be filled with plants, such as Balsams, Cockscombs, &c., that will bear a higher temperature. In general, the rule should be to give air as soon as the thermometer indicates 65°; the maximum heat at noon should never exceed 70°. In cold damp weather a little artificial heat from the flues or hot-water pipes will be of great service.

When the Grapes are fully ripe they will be attacked by wasps and other fruit-eating insects. The best remedy is to cover the air-giving openings with fine netting or canvas. Even a door of canvas will be of service to keep out those intruders. As the Grapes in a greenhouse will hang a long time (till Christmas), the air in the house should be kept as dry as is consistent with the health of the plants. No dead matters should be allowed in the house at all, such as decaying leaves, or moss, or anything that will keep damp. The floors should be kept dry and clean, and abundance of air given during every dry day. Fortunately, all these precautions are equally as necessary for the health of the plants as for keeping the Grapes from moulding and rotting on the Vines.

The Border for Vines in a Greenhouse.—We have already stated how Vine-borders should be drained and made. If it is properly drained, the only covering it will need is one that will keep off the heavy rains during autumn and winter. As the Vines in a greenhouse are not forced, but break naturally with the heat of the spring sun, which heat is applied also to the roots simultaneously, there is no necessity to heat the soil artificially. Early-forced Vines require this, in order that root-action may be going on at the same time that the top-action is set in motion by internal heat.

## VINES IN VINERIES.

The Early Vinery. — *Summer Treatment.* — When Grape Vines have been forced early, so as to have the fruit ripe in May or June, the wood, of course, is ripe early also; and should the summer following be above the average in temperature, there is a great chance that in August or September the buds may break prematurely, and if pushed forward the crop of fruit will come in the following year some time during the month of January or February. To prevent this the cultivator may adopt either of the following methods. If the glass is moveable he should take it off as soon as the last fruit is cut, and expose the Vines to the full influence of the weather, allowing the laterals and end shoots to grow without stopping them, replacing the glass when the nights become colder. This would spend, as it were, the growth, without causing the fruit-bearing buds to break. The growth naturally ceases when the days become shorter, and the nights longer and colder, and thus a perfect rest would be attained in time before the pruning season arrives On the other hand, if the glass is fixed, then the only plan is to give abundance of air night and day, and shade the house from the sun through the summer months to keep the internal air as cool as possible. The shading should be at a little distance from the glass to allow a circulation of air between them, which would keep the glass cool.

*Winter Treatment.* — When very early Grapes are required, then the Vines should be pruned the first week in October, and kept cool for at least six weeks. The forcing then would commence about the middle of November, previous to which the roots should be looked to. If, as recommended, the entire border for this house is inside and heated below, that border should have a good dressing of manure on the surface, and a good soaking of water, and the heat applied underneath. This would cause a commencement of root-action and set the sap in motion. The fires should be lighted then, and the forcing commenced very gradually—45° the first week, 50° the second, and 55° the third, and so keep advancing the temperature till the maximum heat of 70° is reached. By that time the buds will have broken strongly and equally, and may be thinned by disbudding, so as to leave a sufficient number for a fair crop of fruit. A moistish atmosphere should be kept up by syringing the pipes and the Vines in the morning only. The nights are at that season long and often very frosty, and, therefore, a rather drier internal air is to be preferred during the night. Every sunny day give air, being careful that no cold blast rushes in over the young leaves. As soon as the bunches are perceptible, stop the shoot at the joint above the bunch. Keep the shoots tied in to the rafters, but not too closely. The best arrangement is to have three wires, one for the stem, and one on each side to tie the fruit-bearing laterals to. By this time the days will be lengthening and the Vines will come into bloom. At that early season it will be useful to help the setting by giving the wires a sharp shake now and then, in order to disperse the pollen.

With these attentions daily attended to, all things else in proper order, these Vines will bear a fair crop, which ripen about the middle of April or beginning of May.

THE SUMMER VINERY.—The same treatment as to thinning the bunches, stopping laterals, syringing, &c., as that described for Vines in a stove, suits them exactly. In a vinery, however, there is this advantage, that when the fruit is ripe the internal air can be kept drier, because there are no plants to water. As in the case of the earliest vinery, this second house or houses should have plenty of air on all favourable days; but in wet muggy weather a little artificial heat will be useful to dry up the damp that will arise from the internal border. Where convenient, it is a good plan to cover the border with clean slates. Should it be necessary to wash the floors for the sake of cleanliness, it should be done early in the morning when the day is likely to be fine, and the water should be mopped up as dry as possible, that no damp may appear at night. Damp is a great destroyer of ripe Grapes : hence it cannot be too sedulously guarded against. When all the fruit is gathered, then a strong syringing on some fine morning will do good, inasmuch as it will clear the leaves of dust, and bring down any red spider there may be on them. After that the Vines may have a sort of half-pruning—that is, the lower laterals may be cut off, which will let in more light and air to the real fruit-bearing shoots.

*Winter Treatment.*—The winter treatment of Vines that have borne a summer crop of fruit consists in gradually reducing the internal heat as soon as the wood is ripe, half pruning by cutting away the superfluous laterals, and allowing the leaves to fall of their own accord. They may then be pruned, and either tied up to the rafters or brought down to the front and tied in bundles as recommended for Vines in a stove. The vinery may be made use of in winter to shelter half-hardy plants, or bedding-out plants; to preserve which a temperature a few degrees above the freezing point may be kept without any injury to the Vines, only take care to remove them when the Vines require more heat. It is a mistaken notion that the Vine must be subjected to several degrees of frost in order to induce perfect rest.

The Vines in this second house may be started about the end of February, and treated the same as to gentle forcing at first as described above for the early vinery. Remember to clear the stems of the loose bark, and dress them with a composition of sulphur and clay to destroy insects and mildew.

THE LATE VINERY.—The *Summer Treatment* is

simple and easy; all that is required is the usual routine of stopping the laterals, thinning the bunches, &c. As the autumn advances it will be necessary to light the fires, in order to raise the temperature to the proper standard of heat.

*Winter Treatment.*—This house will require heat through the earlier part of winter to ripen the fruit and wood; keep every part dry, and give air on all favourable occasions. By the time the fruit is all gathered winter will be nearly over, and then the Vines should be kept growing through the spring months, and pruned and be put to rest early in the summer, and that rest prolonged as long as possible. They will start into growth, and should be grown on as slowly as possible, in order to cause them to ripen their fruit late in the autumn, and continue in perfection through the winter months. These three successions will, if properly managed, give Grapes for the dessert all the year round.

HEAT.—In all vineries the heat during summer should be, during the day with sun, between 70° and 72°; without sun, 65° to 70° will be sufficient. During the night it may be allowed to fall 5° or 7°. We by no means approve of a low night temperature for the Vine during growth and maturation: neither do we think that a high day temperature is an advantage, but that it is quite the reverse, causing long joints, weak shoots, and abortive buds. Mr. Errington wrote as follows on this point:—

"We may endeavour to give an idea of the air-heat necessary through the spring, first observing that the heat here urged must be understood as independent of immediate sunshine. Let us assume six periods as follows:—

|  | Day. | Night. |
|---|---|---|
| 1. Breaking period to the show of fruit | 55° | 50° |
| 2. Show to the blossoming | 63° | 58° |
| 3. Blossoming to conclusion of first swelling | 70° | 60° |
| 4. Conclusion of first swelling to the conclusion of last swelling | 72° | 60° |
| 5. Ripening period | 65° | 58° |
| 6. Preserving period on the tree | 55° | 50° |

"It may be thought that the night temperature is fixed too low. We do not think so, being assured that much of the complaints about long-jointed wood, bad colouring, &c., &c., have been attributable to an unnatural amount of heat during darkness. The following we think a reasonable and proper advance during sunshine:— Period 2, 10°; 3, 12°; 4, 15°; 5, 10°; 6, 5°.

"Ventilation about as follows:—Period 1, very little; 2, rather liberal; 3, cautiously; 4, very liberal; 5, abundant; 6, abundant during day."

WATERING.—Vines, like everything else, require watering in dry weather, if the roots are as near the surface as they ought to be. If there are few roots within 2 feet of the surface, the watering will be less needed, and if given ever so carefully will have less influence. If, in the latter case, heated water is used, the heat will be absorbed before it reaches the roots; and if manure water is given the virtues of that will be absorbed by the superincumbent soil before getting deep enough. There is, however, just the chance that the heat and the richness will entice the roots upwards. These remarks apply especially to Vines with their roots outside. Of course, when inside the house, waterings must be given as the soil gets dry; and one advantage of having them so planted is, that by judicious, warm, rich waterings, you can, to a certain extent, force the roots as well as the tops. The time of watering Vines with their roots out of doors is a matter of some moment. Could we do as we liked, we would keep all rains and other waterings off Vine-borders outside; at latest after the middle of September, and especially all those that were intended to be forced. No greater mistake exists than the supposition that in these matters gardeners can have their own way if they are fortunate to hold a pretty large situation. The general labouring expenses are so great, that means of keeping borders dry, and yet admitting the sun when it shines, are generally pooh-poohed as unnecessary. We believe that in many small places there are much better means at command for such matters. There can be no question that for such purposes glass, tarpaulin, wooden shutters, and even thatched hurdles, would be extremely useful. By October a little litter could be placed beneath either of these to keep the heat in. With such arrangements the roots will be sure to be moist enough in winter, and yet be comfortably dry instead of being in a wet quagmire condition. For very late houses such means will also be of importance for keeping the Grapes long without damping, if plenty of air, and that moderately dried, is given inside. Such a border, with a dry surface, and covered with dry litter, will not only be warmer all the winter than a moist one, but shortly after shutting up the house for forcing you can at once give a stimulus to root-action by a fair watering with weak liquid manure at a temperature of from 90° to 100°, and that heat will be retained for some time, owing to the dry covering being immediately replaced. Before such watering is given the border should be slightly forked, so as not to injure the roots, and in order that the moisture may sink equally all over it. With such precautions this early watering is of great importance. If the border is exposed it will generally be damp enough, and moderately heated water could have no such influence. Without such precautions, the more moisture given to the border the greater will the amount of cold be by subsequent evaporation; and therefore all waterings given before the end of July ought to be warmer than that obtained from the tank or pond. In order that richness may be imparted by the showers of summer, a covering of horse-droppings, sheep-dung, &c., may be thrown over the border when once the soil is well heated. Our readers will judge whether they can apply a good watering now with advantage. Keeping the above considerations in view, watering can be given at any time; but provided the border is dry in spring, then the three most important times would be when the Vines were nearly starting, when they were setting, and when they commenced their last swelling. We do not approve, however, of the mode of watering some pursue—namely, digging little holes and pouring water in in bucketfuls. We would prefer forking the border, and letting the water percolate through the whole of its width.

## VINES IN POTS.

There are some advantages in cultivating Vines in pots to bear fruit over the ordinary mode of planting them out in borders; and one is, that the pot Vines may be set to rest earlier and more completely by placing them behind a north wall. When Vines in borders are forced early it is always difficult to keep them at rest in the autumn following, especially if it should be a mild one. We have seen them break their best buds in

August or September, and show good bunches of fruit at that untoward season, thus disappointing and tantalising the cultivator; whereas those in pots placed in a cool situation remained quiescent, and could be pruned safely at the proper time. Another advantage is, that those in pots can be brought into the house in succession, and thus in one house the season of fruit-bearing is prolonged almost at pleasure. Vines in pots, too, may be taken out of the house when the fruit is ripe, and placed upon the table. In such a place they are objects of ornament, pleasing the eye as well as the palate. In a bushel of earth a Vine may be planted, and with proper management that Vine will produce several bunches of Grapes in twelve months. Nay, more—a bud from a Vine may be planted in a small pot in January, repotted and grown on, and will ripen fruit in the next season almost as early as the cultivator may please. It is astonishing in how little soil the Vine will grow and be productive. In taking up old Vines we very often find the roots running down close to the wall, seeking food at home instead of wandering away into the rich and scientifically prepared border for them. Bearing these ideas in mind, let no one that has a few square feet of glass despair of being able to grow Grapes.

To return to pot culture, let us remark that one use of growing Vines in pots is to serve as a help to the border-planted Vines. There are many places where the owner may choose to put up one vinery only, and in such a case a few grown in pots will be very useful to produce early Grapes.

If, however, the system of pot culture is practised largely, then a house should be devoted to them entirely. At the vineyard at Garston Mr. Meredith, perhaps, carried this system to a greater extent than anyone else in England.

The kinds to grow in pots are, of *Black-coloured:*—Black Hamburgh (the best of any), Black Prince, Trentham Black, and a few Black Frontignan. *White:*—Royal Muscadine, Dutch Sweetwater, Chasselas Musqué, and one or two Muscat of Alexandria. We recommend a few Muscats, because in pots the quality is excellent.

We have stated that a Vine may be propagated from an eye or bud, and grown on by frequent repottings and applications of liquid manure for one year, and will then be strong enough to bear five or six bunches the following season. This high culture, however, requires so much judgment, carefulness, and extreme attention, that we prefer recommending the young beginner to either grow or procure year-old Vines, and train them to bear fruit the following season. It is a safer and more certain method. Supposing, then, year-old Vines are selected to grow for that purpose, let them be ripened and put to rest as soon as possible, and six weeks previously to commencing growth prune them down to two buds; two are better than one for fear of accidents. Then put them in a rich compost of three parts turfy loam, one part lumpy horse-dung, a few pieces of charcoal, and a little lime rubbish. Mix these together, leaving them in as rough a state as possible. Put them in large pots, rather deeper than ordinary, and from 12 inches to 15 inches wide. Drain well, and put some small bones and inch-square pieces of green turf upon the drainage. Then set in the ball, nearly entire, and pack the compost around it till the pots are full. Press it down firmly, and then it will leave sufficient space to hold water. Commence to grow these in pots as early as convenient, certainly not later than March, in order to obtain ripe wood early in the season. Train them up to within a foot of the glass, and when the shoots are 6 or 7 feet long pinch off the end to strengthen the lower leaves and buds. The uppermost bud will break again, and let it be trained forward 3 or 4 feet further, and then stop it again, and keep the end stopped after that till the year's growth is perfected. The laterals must be stopped at the first leaf, and kept stopped at every succeeding leaf. When the wood begins to turn brown, cut all the laterals off pretty close to the main shoot. If required for a very early crop, the pots should be set out of doors, behind a north wall, in July, and pruned in September. Cut them down in proportion to their strength, or according to the space they will be required to fill; but never exceed 6 or 7 feet in length, however strong the Vines may be.

Now, if you have the convenience, a little bottom heat of 70° or 80° will be useful, but this bottom heat, though certainly beneficial, is not absolutely necessary. The internal heat of the house will answer nearly as well. When the buds break and bunches are visible, stop each shoot close to the bunch, being very careful not to injure the leaf opposite.

The after-treatment is similar to that described for Vines on the rafters in the stove—the stopping the laterals, thinning the bunches, and thinning the berries on each bunch, keeping up a moist atmosphere in the earlier part of the forcing, and a drier atmosphere when the fruit begins to show colour, &c. There is one peculiarity, however, different in pot culture to border culture—and that is, as no wood for the succeeding season is required, all the strength of the Vine may be thrown into that year's crop of fruit. By this it will be understood that we do not recommend fruiting the Vines twice in the same pots. We would rather grow more young Vines and prepare them for bearing the next year, than attempt to get a second crop from those that have borne fruit. Some good gardeners, however, think otherwise, and one writes thus:—

"The question of using young Vines and older Vines is chiefly a matter of convenience and of taste, if the Vines have not been overcropped. This so frequently is the case when Vines are grown in pots, that cultivators generally prefer young Vines to retaining the old ones. Were it not for this overcropping, there is no reason why a Vine in a pot, of good strength, should not produce fruit every year, either by fresh potting, or, rather, by liberal fresh surfacings and manure waterings. The limited quantity of fruit left vigour for wood, and that would be fruitful. When a moderate crop is taken—say from four to six good bunches from a pot some 15 inches in diameter—there will be no great amount of vigour left for wood for next year. We have tried such plants again by growing them the following year, and then fruiting them in the succeeding one; and we tried two methods. By the first we cut down the plant to the lowest bud in the autumn, after the leaves had all fallen; plunged the pot in decayed leaves; placed it in a mild heat in February; and, when the buds were swelling, shook the old soil from the roots, and repotted in rich fibry loam that had been well aired, watered with warm water, and set all growing with a mild bottom heat. Others had the pot examined as to drainage in the autumn; no disrooting or shaking away the soil, but as much of the surface soil as could be removed without hurting the roots taken away, and the place supplied with fresh, rich, fibry soil, kept in a place sheltered from frost during winter, and started again, like the rest, in February; and, if any difference at all, these last made rather the best rods, with the largest, plumpest buds; but there was little difference between them.

"By the second method we left the old fruit-bearing stem, cut every shoot back to the bud nearest the old stem, treated the plants differently by the two modes mentioned above. Still, finding that the pots that had not the earth shaken from the roots did, if anything, rather the best, we, during the summer, allowed each of these spurs to produce a shoot some ten or twelve joints long before stopping it; and using it all the summer with the intention of cutting back to a bud or two in autumn, in order to get fruitful shoots from these the next year. On the whole, costing more trouble, these did no better than those cut down and grown to a single rod. To show that, if very moderately cropped, such Vines would be continuously fruitful, it may be mentioned, that several thus spurred back to make wood only, showed plenty of fruit for a crop. In the case of Vines in pots that bore heavily, say from six to twelve bunches, it was found that they seldom showed at all the following year if spurred in; and that, whatever mode was adopted for growing them without fruit for one summer, they seldom did anything so well as well-ripened young Vines struck from buds inserted in bottom heat at the end of December, and shifted and reshifted as often as they needed it, until they had filled large pots with roots, and had ripened their wood by the beginning of September. We tried several other experiments, such as leaving the old stem when growing on this succession system; picking out all the buds on it, except one or two at the base; and only removing the disbudded stem when the young shoot from its base was growing vigorously, and the stem itself became dried up. The benefit received from such a course might be more imaginary than real; and the thorough investigation of such a subject might easily lead us into questions beyond our full comprehension. There can be no question that Vines in pots, well managed and very moderately cropped, may produce every year. When cropped moderately, or a little extra moderately, there will be little difficulty in getting the same plants to fruit one season, and produce wood the next, for fruiting the third season. And when very heavily cropped, our impression is, that young plants grown vigorously, with all the necessary adjuncts of bottom heat, &c., will beat old ones. The growing of Vines in pots is chiefly to be looked upon as auxiliary, when mere profit is concerned; but when grown on from buds, there are few matters of practice more absorbingly interesting."

THE COILING SYSTEM.—Some years ago Mr. Mearns startled the Vine-growing world by asserting that a long branch might be cut off a Vine inserted in a pot, and made to produce fruit the following season, just the same as if it had remained on the parent stem. This he proved might be done by what he called the "coiling system;" and he certainly did achieve that effect. The necessary materials are good, healthy, long shoots of the Vine, large pots to hold them, and bottom heat to plunge the pots in whilst the tops of the coils are in a cool atmosphere.

It often happens that Vines are from some cause or other obliged to be cut down. Taking it for granted that such is the case with one or more of our readers, and that he or they, instead of throwing the branches or stems away, should like to try the coil system, let him choose such as are flexible, with a good yearling shoot at the end; then prune off all the lower laterals, but not too close, leaving the leading shoot from 2 to 5 feet long in proportion to its strength. Then have ready as many pots, 15 inches in diameter, as there are shoots for the experiment. Drain well, covering the drainage with fresh-cut turf chopped in inch-square pieces, and upon them put a small quantity of a compost of half-decayed turf three parts, and one part of hotbed dung, well mixed, adding some pieces of charcoal and old lime rubble. After that place the lower end of the shoot down to this layer of soil, and begin to coil the shoot round the pot side, filling in the soil as the coiling proceeds, and coil away up to the top of the pot, leaving out the length of last year's shoot. Tie this to an upright stick, and then proceed with another branch, and so on till all are coiled and tied to the sticks.

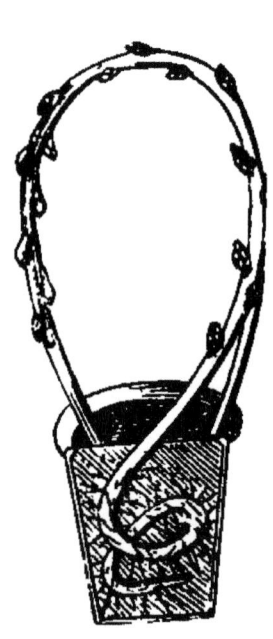

Fig. 17.

In places where leaves are collected in quantities, form them into a bed, and plunge the coiled shoots in their pots amongst the leaves. The heat of the leaves will cause roots to be emitted the whole length of the branches or stems that are buried in the pot. They may, indeed, be termed monster cuttings. The young shoots being in a low temperature will remain quiet. By thus obtaining roots first, the shoots will be ready to start with vigour whenever they are removed into a higher temperature. Place the pots when convenient into a house, beginning first with a temperature of about 45°, and very greatly increase that heat as the shoots begin to develope foliage; afterwards treat them the same as to moisture, stopping the laterals, thinning, &c., as described before for Vines in pots. If all has been well and judiciously managed, these coiled Vine shoots will produce a fair crop of fruit the following year. If leaves to make a gentle hotbed to start the branches into rooting are not at hand, the same effect may be attained by making a hotbed of stable litter, with a good deep bed of spent tanners' bark upon it. The only point to attend to is not to make this dung-bed too strong; the bottom heat should not exceed 80°.

## VINES IN THE OPEN AIR ON WALLS.

In the south of England we often see the walls of cottages and even better-class houses covered with a Vine, which in favourable seasons ripens very good fruit, or, at least, would do so if better managed: for usually every bunch the Vine shows is allowed to grow, and not a berry is thinned out; and too often not a summer's shoot is shortened; and the training is just haphazard. With such management it is no wonder that the fruit is not so good as it might be if better attended to.

If a Vine is planted against a house the main stem should be trained straight up, and side shoots trained from it to cover the spaces between the windows. Young wood should be laid in annually and brought close to the wall to ripen it, and no more should be allowed than is necessary to produce fruit. All laterals should be stopped at the first joint and cut away as the wood ripens. Regular attention to this stopping and training, and allowing no more than one bunch to each shoot, and as soon as the berries are as large as peas to thin out at least half of them, would give the fruit a chance to swell larger and ripen better.

Fig. 18.

It is, however, to the culture of the Grape Vines on a garden wall facing the south, that we have to draw the attention of the cultivator. The management, after the border is properly made and the Vine planted, consists chiefly in pruning and training. The best mode of training is, first to obtain two shoots from the two buds left on when the Vine was planted. Let them be trained upright at 2 feet apart (*fig.* 18). Then in the autumn bring those two shoots down, and train them horizontally at about half a yard from the ground (*fig.* 19). Pinch out all the buds excepting three on each side of the main stem. Let these six shoots be trained perpendicularly close to the wall (*fig.* 20). If all has gone on well, those shoots will run up to the top of the wall that year. During the summer stop all the laterals at the first joint, and stop each leading

Fig. 19.

shoot when it has reached the top of the wall. See that the shreds are not too tight. If the summer is dry give the border a good soaking of water once a fortnight. The distance from shoot to shoot should be 2½ feet. If they are closer the

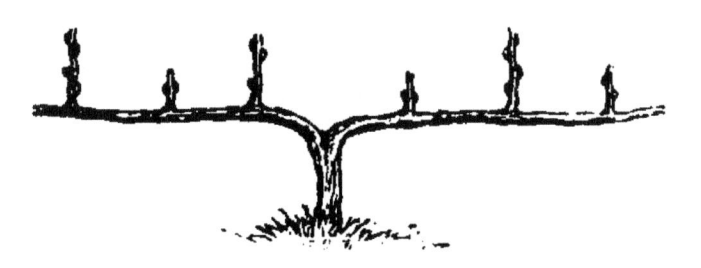

Fig. 20.

wood will not ripen well, and if wider there would be a loss of space. By the end of September or the middle of October the leaves should be turning yellow and the wood brown. As soon as the first frost has brought off all the leaves, then proceed to prune the Vines.

*Pruning on the Long-Rod System.* —By this plan a regular supply of good fruit-bearing wood is secured, and, besides that, the method is simple, and is regular and neat in appearance. In the autumn the Vines will have two shoots to bear

Fig. 21.

fruit, and these should be trained to nearly the top of the wall. Two others will be cut down to a bud close to the main horizontal stems. These will send up shoots to be trained between the fruit-bearers, whilst the two end shoots should be trained down in the same line as the horizontal ones.

In the third summer the last year's horizontally-trained shoots should have all the buds rubbed off, excepting two on each. These two should be 2½ feet apart, and, trained to the wall, should reach the top of it that year. This year's growth will cover the space of wall each Vine should fill—that is, there will be four fruit-bearing upright shoots, and four shoots to bear fruit the following year (*fig.* 21). In the autumn those that have borne fruit should be cut down, and the others left nearly their own length to bear fruit.

Should the Vines when four or five years old be of weakly growth, then remove a portion of the surface soil, and add a sufficient quantity of fresh compost to renew and sustain their strength. Occasional watering with liquid manure will greatly assist their growth, and will help to swell off the fruit. The finest fruit will always be near the top of the wall.

The following are good kinds to grow against a wall in the open air:—Early Black July, Miller's Burgundy (black), Black Hamburgh, Royal Muscadine (white), Dutch Sweetwater, and Early Ascot Frontignan.

The *alternate mode of pruning* the Vine may be varied to suit circumstances. The same principle is that called *horizontal training*. A main stem is carried up to the top of the wall, and side shoots at regular intervals are trained at right angles from it (*fig.* 22).

This plan answers admirably for Vines trained against the walls of a dwelling-house, and also against a wall purposely set apart for Vines. In the latter case the shoots may be trained and pruned yearly just on the alternating principle—

that is, one shoot to bear fruit, and another to produce wood alternately with each other.

The *spur pruning* is almost as simple as the other. Furnish the wall with upright or horizontal shoots, and prune in annually the laterals, which should not be left too numerous, to a single eye or bud. When these buds break they

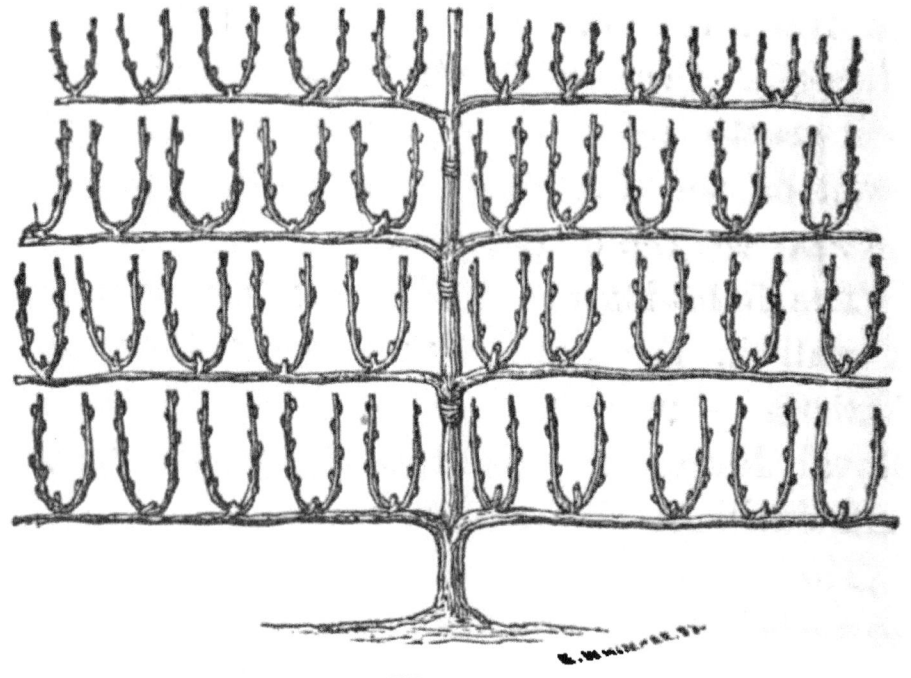

Fig. 22.

should be all trained on the upper side of the branch (*fig.* 23), and not pointing upwards, but rather aslant, so as to allow the bunch to hang clear of the stem that bears the fruit.

*Summer Treatment.*—This comprises stopping the fruit-bearing laterals one joint beyond the bunch, and stopping also the side laterals at the first joint. This stopping must be persevered in all the summer. Each lateral that bears fruit should be fastened to the wall in its early stage, in order that it may not be broken off by the wind or its own weight. Never allow more than one bunch to a shoot, and thin the bunches moderately to allow the berries that are left room to swell. Should the season prove a dry one, then

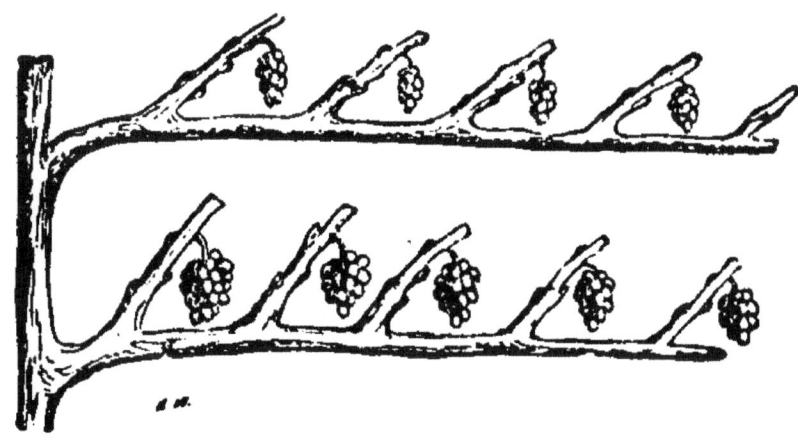

Fig. 23.

give the border a good watering once a week, and every third time water with liquid manure of a moderate strength. Syringe the Vines as soon as the fruit is set to keep the leaves clear of dust. Do this in the evening; then the leaves and fruits will get dry before the sun has any power to injure. Cease syringing as soon as the Grapes begin to colour. Of course in rainy weather the syringing will be dispensed with. Should mildew appear, dust it directly with flowers of sulphur, which will check the disease if taken in time. When the fruit is all gathered, then cut off all supernumerary laterals and leaves, to allow the sun to heat the wall, and thereby ripen the wood.

In wet cold summers, however, the wood may possibly not get ripened to the full length of the yearling shoots to the top of the wall, especially in situations considerably north of London. In such a case (or indeed in every case for the Vine) the wall should be flued and heated either by the old method of common hot air, heated from a fire placed at the north side, or by hot-water pipes carried within the flues in the wall to the top, with returning pipes brought down again to the boiler. The advantages of hot-water pipes are that the top part of the wall will be equally or nearly warm as the lowest range, which is not so with walls heated with the smoke or hot air in the ordinary flues. In addition to this helping the Vine to ripen its wood by heating the wall, the ripening of the fruit will be assisted also. In unfavourable summers, if the cultivator has a few spare lights of glass at hand, he might with advantage make use of them by placing them against his Grape wall. Even covering the bunches of fruit with bell or small hand-lights, suspended against the wall as in *fig.* 24, would ripen the fruit better and sooner than if left fully exposed.

Fig. 24.

Copings.—We advise the use of wide copings; they arrest the hoar frosts of spring and autumn, as also the radiation or loss at night of heat which had accumulated during the day. They moreover serve to protect the fruit after it is ripe, and they enable the operator to suspend any protective covering with ease; in fact, if half a yard wide, we do not see why they may not be made to produce a real conservative wall, after the manner of Chatsworth and some other places; we mean by having a curtain of some material to slide along a rod.

In order to facilitate the growth and ripening of both the wood and fruit, early shelter from late spring frosts and cold winds is necessary; the wall should therefore be covered with netting. Much has been said in favour of tiffany; but though it has merits, yet, from its close texture, it excludes too much light and air. Woollen netting also holds moisture too long, and contracts and expands according to the state of the weather. However, any of these kinds are sufficiently good for the purpose, and, used early in the season, will help to bring out the young shoots earlier, and protect them from cold. Remove these shelters towards the end of May. In the autumn, if it should be cold and wet, then replace the shelters, for the double purpose of ripening the fruit and the wood.

The woodcuts, *figs*. 22 and 23, show how the side shoots or laterals should be trained so as to give the bunches clear space to swing, as it were, at their ease. In such an open position the sun will heat the wall in their immediate neighbourhood, and thus conduce to mature and ripen them better than if they were hanging close to the stems in a thicket of leaves.

Ringing.—Vines grown on the long-rod system we have seen ringed with very decided advantage. Mr. Weaver writes thus upon this application of the " Ring of Pomona: "—

"No Vines cultivated on any other system are so capable of being ringed, without the disadvantage of killing or losing the future useful part of the tree; because on Hoare's or long-rod system the whole of the previous year's bearers will have to be cut entirely away.

"The very right time to perform this ringing is just after the berries are all set, or have attained the size of No. 2 shot, or small peas. In ringing cut with a sharp knife clean round the branch between two joints. Or, if you are going to ring the laterals carrying the fruit, leave either two or three buds and leaves beyond the main stem, and make the ring just in the middle, between the third and fourth leaves or joints. As I said before, make two cuts clean through the bark quite down into the wood, one inch apart, and remove the bark clean away all round the branch or lateral. By this means, if you are in the habit of spur-pruning, the hinder buds are left all right to spur back to the following year. If you prune upon the long-rod system, you may ring the rod just wherever you please—the whole branch, if you like—as this ringed part will have to be cut away entirely after the fruit is gathered.

"The ringing is performed just the same on an old whole branch as in that of the young lateral carrying one or two bunches. I have repeatedly ringed old branches, that have been carrying from twenty to thirty bunches of Grapes, with the same good effect; only it has been such branches that I have intended to cut entirely away the following autumn. Of course, thinning out the berries of the bunches, and the bunches too if excellence is to be aimed at, is of the utmost importance. The process of thinning cannot be too early attended to. I always begin as soon as the fruit is fairly set, and continue to remove all inferior berries, and this with a good pair of scissors and clean fingers—using my eyes to see what I am about, so as not to injure the berries by handling and mauling them.

"By thus practising ringing I have produced, for the last twelve or fourteen years, Grapes out of doors that have puzzled many a tyro, and others too.

"It must not be done in a hesitating timid manner. There must be a ring of bark perfectly removed; the cuts being made boldly down to the very young wood, or alburnum, and every particle of bark, inner and outer, must be removed between the cuts.

"*Fig.* 25 represents faithfully the ringed part of a rod at the close of autumn, and shows how the removal of the band of bark checked the return of the sap, and how, in consequence, the rod above the removed band increased in size beyond that portion of the rod below the band.

"The effect upon the berries was in every instance to advance their early ripening a fortnight, and to about double the size and weight of the berries when compared with those grown on unringed branches of the same Vine. Nor was the colour and bloom of the berries diminished; indeed, so excellent were they, that we have seen them exhibited deservedly by the side of Grapes grown under glass, and they were sold in November at Winchester for half-a-crown a pound."

Fig. 25.

## GROUND OR CURATE'S VINERY.

In Mr. Rivers's little volume, "The Miniature Fruit Garden," occurs the following description of what he terms "The Curate's Vinery:"—

"The annexed figure (*fig.* 26), will convey a correct idea of its shape and make. To form a vinery of this description, some dry place in

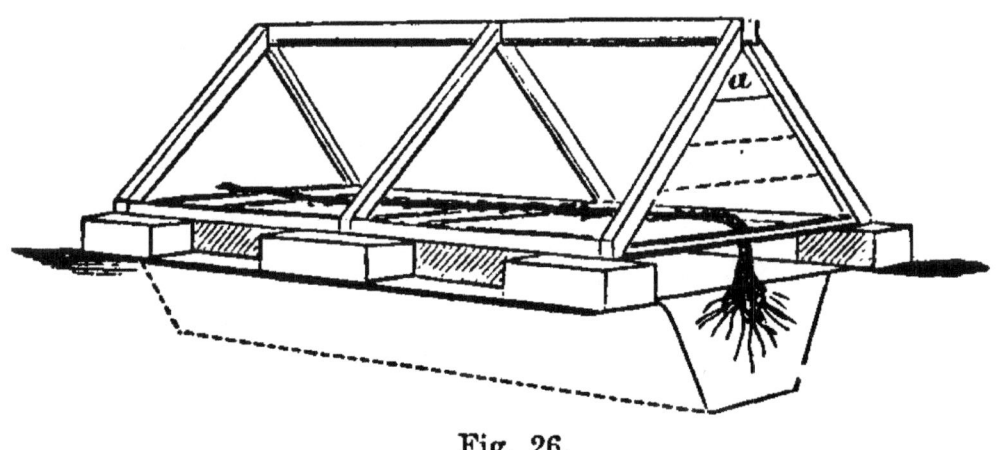

Fig. 26.

the garden must be selected; if not naturally so, it must be well drained. A dry, gravelly, or sandy border, gently sloping to the south or south-west, will be found a favourable site; a flat surface will, however, do well if fully exposed to the sun.

"When the site is determined on, a trench should be dug 2 feet wide on the surface, and 15 inches deep, sloping on each side to the bottom, which should be 6 inches wide; the bottom must be paved with tiles placed lengthwise, and the sides lined with the slates called duchesses, also placed lengthwise.

"On each side of this trench, on the surface of the soil, a row of bricks must be placed 2 inches apart, end to end, leaving spaces between each brick 2 inches wide; these are for ventilation. On these two rows of bricks the roof is to be placed, which would be a ridge of the following dimensions:—2 feet 6 inches wide at bottom, and 15 inches deep from the centre to the apex. It should be made in lengths of 7 feet, two of which, placed end to end, form one vinery 14 feet long. Each length should be glazed with four pieces of glass; and as each sloping side of the ridge is 20 inches deep, four pieces of glass about 20 inches square for each side will be required. The two outer ends must be closed with board; at one end a notch should be cut in the board to admit the stem of the Vine, which should be planted outside, so that its stem is on a level with the surface of the soil outside; the soil the Vine is planted in should be well stirred, 2 feet deep, over a space 6 feet square, and enriched with rotten manure, and what are called one-inch bones or 'bone-dust.' The Vine, when planted, should be introduced and suffered to grow as in a common vinery till it reaches the end. Pruning on the spur system is the only method to be followed. To support the Vine in the centre, pieces of slight iron rod should be placed across the furrow, 2 feet apart, resting on the surface outside; to these the stem of the Vine should be fastened, so as to be under the centre of the roof. The bunches of Grapes will thus hang in the centre of the furrow, and, owing to the radiation of heat from the slates and tiles, they will ripen well. I need scarcely mention that in pruning, either in winter or summer, the two lengths of ridge forming the roof must be taken off and replaced when the operation is finished. Owing to the moisture from the soil, red spider but rarely makes its appearance; but it will be a sure preventive if flowers of sulphur are kept thickly sprinkled on the slates and tiles during the months of June and July. It is not only for Vines that these strictly-called ridge-and-furrow vineries are adapted—Pears on the quince stock, and Peaches and Nectarines, all cultivated as closely-pruned pyramids, may be grown in them: the latter would require to be lifted annually in November to keep down excessive vigour. A seven-feet length, closed at one end, should be appropriated to one tree, the open end towards the root.

"Their cost for carpentry, as given by my village builder, is 6s. 6d. for each seven-feet length; glass about 4s. So that a vinery for one Vine will cost, including slates and bricks, about 25s.

"There are several garden purposes to which these simple structures may be applied. I fill my trench half full of rich mould early in November, and plant in it Endive and Cabbage Lettuces for winter and early spring salads.

"In gardens where these glazed ridge-roofs are not wanted for Vines or fruit-tree culture, they will be found most useful. They may be placed on any warm border on the surface of the soil, and early Peas, French Beans, and many other early vegetables requiring protection from spring frosts be grown under them with advantage. In all cases they should be placed on bricks, with spaces between them. Ventilation is then secured; and even Cauliflower plants in winter will do well without the constant attention to 'giving air,' so necessary in the old garden-frame culture. In gardens that are confined and very warm, it may be necessary to have the ends not quite closed up, at a small opening left at the top, at *a* in the figure, just under the ridge, to let out the heated air. My vinery stands in a very exposed place, and has not required it."

In reference to the foregoing we have received the following from Mr. Rivers:—

"I send you a slight modification of that

humble vinery, which I find simple, eligible, and agreeable, and likely to supersede the original form.

"It was one day, about the end of June last, that I found myself looking into my original 'Curate's Vinery,' and admired the Vines then in blossom, although those within a few yards of it, growing in the open air, were scarcely in full leaf. I pictured to myself the bunches of Grapes suspended from the Vines in the warm moist atmosphere of the trench lined with slates. My thoughts then reverted to my boyish Grape-loving days, when in an old vineyard planted by my grandfather, I always looked for some ripe Grapes about the end of September; and I vividly remembered that I always found the best and ripest bunches with the largest berries lying on the ground, and if the season were dry and warm, they were free from dirt, and *de*licious (I think I always strongly accented the *de*); and so I gradually travelled in thought from bunches of Grapes lying on the ground to *idem* lying on slates.

"The idea was new, and I commenced at once to put it into practice by building a 'Curate's Vinery' on a new plan.

"I therefore placed rows of bricks endwise (leaving 4 inches between each brick for ventilation), on a nice level piece of sandy ground, and then paved between them with large slates ('duchesses') placed crosswise. On the bricks I placed two of the ridges of glass, as given in the foregoing figure, each 7½ feet long, and thus formed my vinery 15 feet in length. One Vine will in the course of two years fill a vinery of this length; but to reap the fruits of my project quickly I planted two Vines, one in the centre the other at the north-east end; for these structures should stand north-east and south-west. One of these Vines, which had been growing in a pot in the open air, was just beginning to show its fruit-buds—it was quite the last of June—its fruit are now fully coloured and quite ripe. I therefore feel tolerably well assured that Grapes lying on a floor of slates, such as I have described, will ripen from two to three weeks earlier than in vineries of this description with a furrow, and as much earlier than Grapes in a common cold vinery. Black Hamburghs and other kinds of Grapes not requiring fire heat may thus be grown in any small garden at trifling expense. I am indeed inclined to think that the Frontignans, and nearly all but the Muscats, may be ripened by this method, so intense is the heat of the slated floor on a sunny day in July.

"Some persons may think that the heat would be scorching, and that leaves and Grapes would alike become frizzled; but few gardeners know the extreme heat a bunch of Grapes can bear. I remember a lady friend, who had resided some time at Smyrna, telling me that one afternoon at the end of summer, when the Grapes were ripening, she was sitting in her drawing-room and admiring some large bunches of Grapes hanging on a Vine which was growing against the wall in the full sunshine. Knowing the danger of going into the open air without a parasol, she rushed out, cut a bunch of Grapes, and returned to her seat in the shady room. The bunch of Grapes was so hot that she was obliged to shift it from hand to hand. I observed in the hot weather we had in July last year, one or two bunches of Muscat Grapes nearly touching the chimney of the stove in which a fire was kept up every morning, gradually turning into raisins. I felt them when the sun was shining on them: they were not burning hot, but next to it. I allowed them to dry into raisins, and very fine they were, but not better than the finest imported from Spain.

"With respect to the superior ripening power of slates or tiles placed on the surface of the earth, I was much interested in once hearing a travelled friend say that, when he was at Paros, he observed many Vines trained up the marble rocks peculiar to the island; and in all cases the Grapes lying on the surface, which was almost a continuous mass of rock, were ripe, while those a few feet from it, on the same Vine, some of the branches of which were trained up the wall-like rocks, were quite green. In telling me this he said he was never more impressed with the ripening power of the earth's surface.

"I have, in giving the figure and description of the 'Curate's Vinery,' made it adapted for one Vine, the width of it being 2 feet 6 inches only. If this width be increased to 3 feet 6 inches two Vines can be trained under the same roof, and thus, at a trifling additional cost, double produce can be obtained. I have very recently planted some Peach-trees in one of these slate-paved vineries, and feel assured that very early and very fine Peaches can be grown in such places. I have managed my trees in this way— I took two pyramids full of blossom-buds, cut off the shoots on one side, so that the stem would lie flat, and I then pegged it down with hooks made of stout iron wire, thrusting them into the soil between the interstices of the slates.

"Cultivators will think of red spider making his home in such (for him) a happy, hot place; but it may be made so uncomfortable by keeping flowers of sulphur strewed over the slates till near the ripening season, that no inconvenience need be apprehended. It will be perceived that the ventilation is all lateral, and on the same principle as that of my orchard-houses; nothing can be more perfect. In the figure of the 'Curate's Vinery,' with a furrow, it will be seen I have left a small aperture under the apex of the roof for the escape of rarefied air. In my paved vineries I have not done this, and yet the ventilation is perfect. I have not yet ascertained in what manner the heated air escapes. The ventilating apertures are all on the surface of the soil, and at the same level; but I suppose it stoops to get out, having no other mode of egress.

"I ought to add that a 'Curate's Vinery' for Peach-trees need be but 10 feet long, in two five-feet lengths."

A lean-to ground vinery, with a one-inch board for the back, would do very well; but it should be placed on bricks, so as to be properly ventilated, and the sloping glass roof should be facing the south or south-west—in fact, such a structure would be very cheap, more easily made, and quite as efficient as the ridge-shaped roof. The back wall or board of such a vinery should be 18 or 20 inches high, its front from 6 to 8 inches. Grapes would ripen well in such structures, and for ground on the incline they would be more convenient than ridge ground vineries.

We have a lean-to ground vinery 26 feet long, 2½ feet high at the back, and 2 feet at the base, with four Vines in it. One is planted at each end, and two in the middle. These are trained in opposite directions along stout galvanised-iron wires stretched from end to end of the vinery. The glass is in seven lights, like those of Cucumber-frames, and they are lifted on and off by handles.

## VINES ON TRELLISES.

The first season a trellis is not absolutely required, beyond a temporary support to keep the Vine off the ground; still it is not objectionable in most instances to have it erected at once, and it should always be done before the roots extend too much, so as not to interfere in setting the stakes or posts for general support, as no good can come in displacing or bruising the roots in the operation. It will be required early in the second season's growth, and a few months gained never come amiss. We shall not speak at any length, or describe the practice of some, of using stake supports. We have never seen it giving good satisfaction in this climate, and it usually has been abandoned, so far as our observation goes. A trellis 6 feet high is sufficient, usually constructed by setting posts at either end of the row of Vines, with one between each of the Vines planted; upon this nail strips of board 1½ inch wide, and 15 inches apart from the bottom upwards. This makes a cheap trellis, both in first cost and durability. It is better to set posts as above, omitting every alternate one except at the ends, taking pains to select such timber as will prove most durable. Work them down to a neat and tasty size (4 to 6 inches), facing one side, except for the end ones, which may be round. A man's habits in taste are easily read about the grapery, and nothing contributes more to the well-being and appearance of a garden than a light, airy, and durable trellis. Number 8 wire, drawn horizontally the same distance apart as though of wood, and attached to the posts by passing through them at the ends, and fastened to the others by staples formed from pieces of the same wire, but not so tight but that the wire can play horizontally, will be found much more durable; and where the extended trellis is wished, upon which to train long horizontal arms

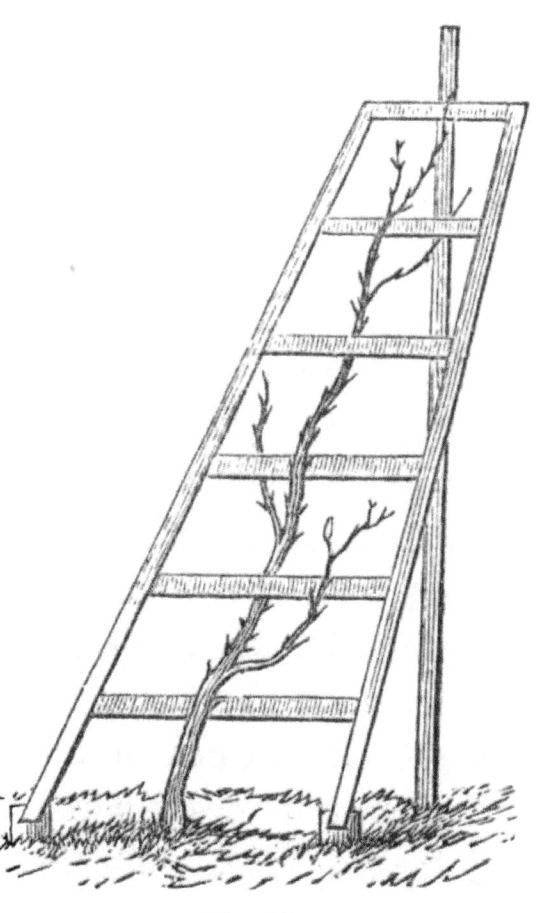

Fig. 27.

of the Vine, as good, if not the best mode of construction. In short seasons, changeable climate, and frosty localities, something more is often desirable than the immoveable support, upon which the Vine, once attached, must remain till autumn, or with much difficulty be removed. The figure (*fig.* 27) illustrates a trellis well adapted for the protection of the Vine in the event of late spring frosts, as it affords good opportunities for covering. It consists of two posts 3 feet long, set in the ground upon either side of the Vine, and 6 feet apart equal distance therefrom, with 6 inches above the ground, and pin-holes near the tops for attaching the frame, which is made of two-by-four scantling, 6 feet long, with corresponding pin-holes; or, what is preferable, use strap hinges for attachments, and then, when the frame is erected, it will rest upon the posts and not on the pins. Upon the scantling fasten cross-bars half an inch thick by 2 inches wide, embedded their thickness in the frame. The whole tapers to 3 feet at the top, which is supported by a moveable lever or part to any height required, and may be as readily changed from a horizontal position for covering up, to an upright position for exposure to the sun, as the blade of a knife may be opened and shut upon its handle. The bars being placed upon alternate sides, the Vines can be passed between them, thus needing no other support by tying or otherwise.

## RAISING AND REPLANTING VINES.

According to circumstances Vines may be taken up at any time, if extra trouble is no consideration. For instance: we have removed the soil from a part of a border of Vines in January and March, and added fresh to the roots that were moved with care; but we should greatly have preferred doing that work in the months of September and October, but we could not get at them then. We have partly disearthed Vines in the end of June, shaded the tops until tops and roots were growing afresh, then removed nearly the whole of the wood and grew fresh wood; that ripened well, and produced a heavy crop the following May. Here, however, to gain time, there was much extra labour in shading and syringing, so as to prevent a leaf shrivelling or flagging until the reciprocal action between roots and branches was restored.

In general, however, the end of September would be the best time for performing such an operation with the earliest of these houses, as by that time the wood for next season would be pretty well matured, and the fruit be cut, and yet there would be a sufficiency of green leaves and fresh growth on the Vines. That, provided a fair amount of shade were given, would encourage immediate root-action into the warm soil before the chilling nights came on, and the following season the Vines would break with little abated vigour. All things considered, this would be the most suitable time for practitioners under general circumstances. The shading and care at that time would be a trifle to what it would be in May or June. The next best, and what would involve least trouble, would be to wait until the leaves were getting yellow—say the middle of October. No shading would then be required; and provided the border was covered with dry litter, there would still be enough heat in the soil to encourage fresh root-action. The worst time of all would be winter or early spring, if you expected much the following summer.

By lifting the Vines in early summer, the wood formed afterwards will be changed in its character. That will also partly be the case if the roots are raised early in autumn. If raised rather late in autumn, the bearing wood for next year will not be much influenced as to productiveness, though the fruit, most likely, will be saved from shanking and wiring; but the chief benefit will be found in the second year, as respects wood and fruit. If the Vines are lifted in winter and spring, unless great counteracting care is exercised in the way of artificial heat, both wood and fruit will be likely to suffer the first season, and it will be the second before the full benefit appears, and that only if care is taken to lessen the checks unavoidably given.

As to *cutting* back the Vines when lifted, what has been said on pruning will equally apply to them. For instance: raise Vines in June; keep, as advised, every leaf and shoot inside that is green, until the roots are working vigorously afresh. If the Vine is furnished well from top to bottom, we might keep and mature the wood it has, taking off the shading by dgrees; but in general it will be preferable, after the roots are acting freely, to cut back the Vines considerably and depend on new growth. Either plan will do, according to circumstances. In lifting in early autumn, you may prune as you like as soon as the leaves get yellow. In lifting later, you may cut the tops before you lift, or after; it matters little, but the first would be the best.

Recollect, the roots must not be *dug* up. The work must be commenced at the outside of the border by sinking a deep trench there below the roots, and working the face of the bank down carefully with a pick and fork, so as to save all the roots of any size. These roots should also be kept from a drying air, and kept moist until replanted. Much has been said of draining and forming borders. New soil of a rough loamy nature will be best, and a few bones will be the most lasting manure.

## DISEASES.

SHANKING.—This disease is a sort of ulcer or gangrene on the footstalks of the bunches, causing that part to decay, and, consequently, rendering it useless. The cause of this is, we believe, the soil being too cold during the time of growth—the sap rises too slowly for the rapid growth in the warm vinery: hence, the Vine being deficient in sap, some parts must suffer, and the most tender parts, the footstalks of the blossoms, show it first. If the roots are examined when shanking appears, they will be found discoloured and unhealthy. The remedy will be easily suggested—let the soil be warmed, and then the action will be congenial between the leaves and roots.

BUNCHES CURLING.—When this occurs the best remedy is to tie a stone or other weight to the end of the bunch, sufficient to keep it straight.

LEAVES SHANKED.—We once saw Vine leaves thus affected. Their upper surface was slightly mildewed, but the stalks were completely gangrened, like the stalks of Grapes when shanked. The consequence was that the leaves then dry up as if scalded. We attribute this disease to the same cause as shanking — viz., the roots getting into an ungenial subsoil; or, from being chilled outside the house, are not able to supply sap sufficient to support the growth taking place within the house. Keeping the house cooler and giving more air, whilst the roots are kept warmer and supplied with liquid manure, would probably remove the evil. Vine-shoots also gangrene. We think the cause of the ends of a Vine's young shoots "fogging-off" or gangrening is that the roots have descended into a cold or ungenial soil. We would remove the soil down to the first tier of roots, and replace it with a mixture of equal parts light loam and decayed stable manure. If the roots are outside the house cover the surface with mulch at night and during cold days, but have it uncovered during sunny days and warm rains.

LEAVES WARTED.—This is not a disease, but excrescences, the result of too much moisture at the roots, and a too close moist atmosphere inside. Extra drainage if needed, and especially a drier and more airy atmosphere, are the remedies.

SHRIVELLING is when the berries do not swell equally. Frequently the lower parts of the bunch will be totally lost, and the berries remain stationary and become sour; they then shrivel up, and are, of course, worthless. Like shanking, this disease arises from the state of the border. The effectual remedy is to lift the Vines when at rest, make a new border in the proper manner, and replant the Vines if not too old, laying the roots in not deeper than 9 inches from the surface, and warming the soil, either by a heated chamber underneath, or by a covering of old leaves and littery dung, sheltering it at the same time from heavy cold rains or snow by canvas or a covering of boards, or even thin turf laid all over it closely.

THE SPOT. — This disease attacks the berries only, and is akin to shanking. The Canon Hall Muscat is peculiarly liable to this complaint. It is caused, no doubt, partly by the state of the roots and also by sudden changes of the temperature inside. The remedy is obvious : put the roots in a right temperature, watch the vicissitudes of the change of the external atmosphere, and in giving air see that the cold air does not rush through upon the fruit; and lastly, let the fruit be shaded from the rays of the sun, either by the natural shade afforded by the leaves, or by a shading outside of netting.

RUST. — This is sometimes supposed to have been brought on by handling the berries during the thinning process, or by the operator's hair coming in contact with the berries; but as, if neither of those supposed causes have happened, still the rust appears, we believe it arises from a too high temperature given whilst the fruit is small, causing a too rapid accumulation of sap, which the skin cannot swell fast enough to receive: hence it is necessary always to force mode-

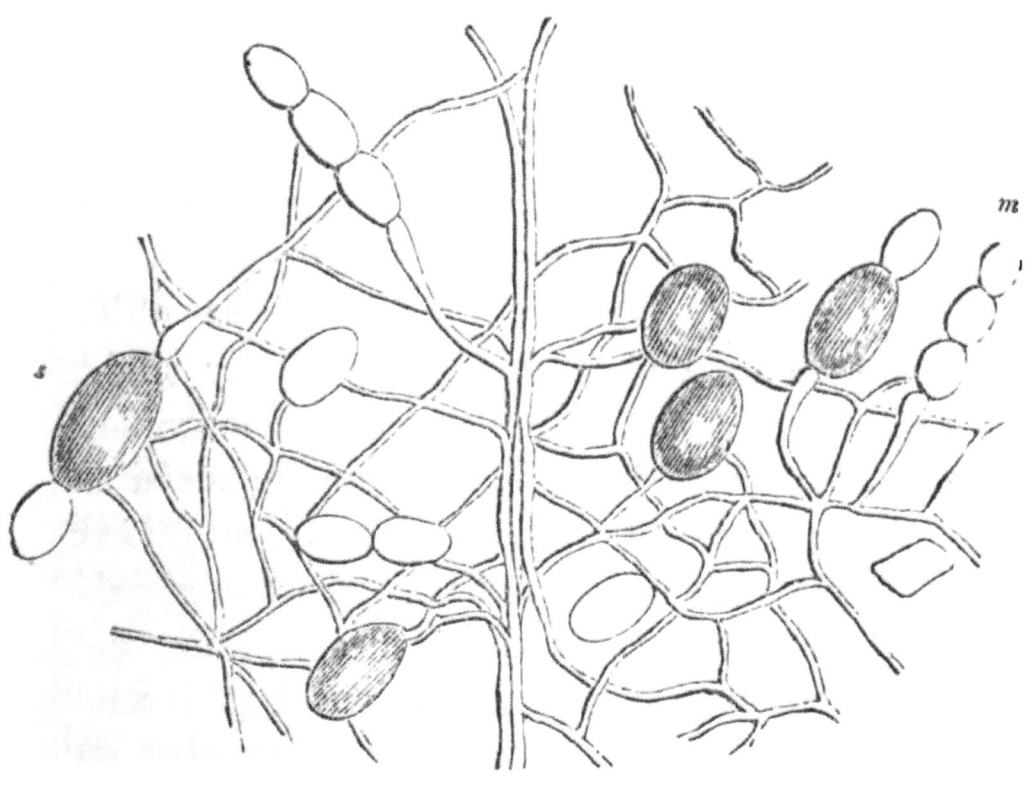

Fig. 28.

rately. The old proverb, "Too much haste the less speed," applies to forcing fruits as well as any other pursuit in life.

MILDEW.—Perhaps of all the diseases to which the Vine is liable, this is the most formidable. If examined by the microscope it will be seen to be a form of the small fungi or mushroom tribe, the roots of which penetrate the epidermis, sucking out, as it were, the juices, and stopping the healthy respiration. *Fig.* 28 represents a small portion of the surface of a Grape, on which the cryptogam has spread itself, magnified to 300 diameters. From the mycelium arise moniliform filaments (*m*), and the sporangia (*s*). Two of the latter have an utricle directly attached to their upper extremity. In *fig.* 29 the sporangium is represented magnified to 600 diameters, and by its side are the spores it has emitted, which, taken separately, are as transparent as white glass; seen in a mass they have a very slight yellow tint. In *fig.* 30 are three spores magnified to 1800 diameters, in order to show the nuclei or globules at their extremities. *Fig.* 31, magnified 1000 diameters, shows at *x* three utricles in germination. At *y* are two fresh utricles, showing the little globules and the mucilaginous liquid contained in them. At *z* is an utricle shrivelled up by lateral compression, which has given rise to the optical illusion of a longitudinal slit.

When the mildew does appear upon the Vine leaves, or Grapes, let all the parts be gently rubbed between the thumb and fingers, kept well covered with flowers of sulphur by dipping them into a plate or bag of those flowers. The sulphur must not be washed off by syringing or other application of water. Let it continue on until it falls off, or until the fruit is ripe. When cut, a dewing by the aid of the very finest rose of the syringe will entirely remove the sulphur, but leave the bloom upon the Grapes.

It would be very interesting to trace out the

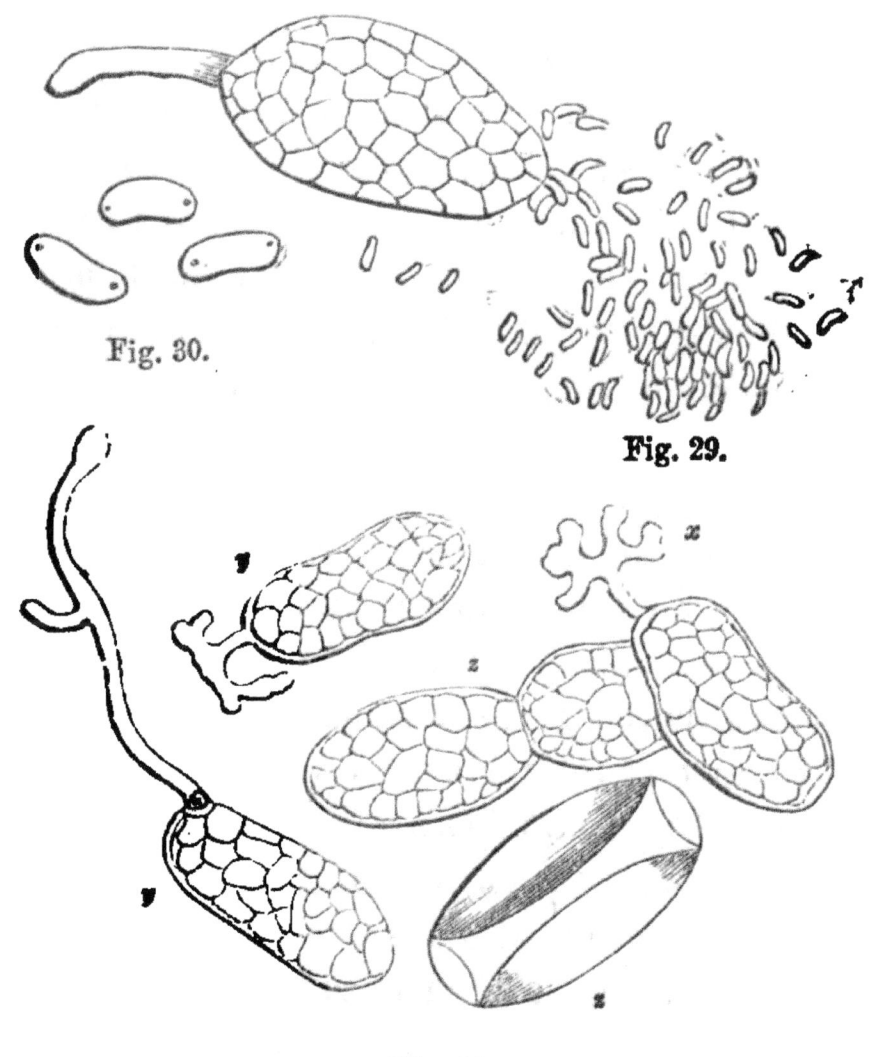

Fig. 30.

Fig. 29.

Fig. 31.

birthplace of the Vine mildew. We have an impression that it first appeared in Germany in the year 1845; it reached England, being first noticed at Margate in 1847. Its fungal nature was pointed out by Mr. Tucker, gardener to J. Slater, Esq., of that town. The Rev. M. J. Berkeley decided that it is a new species of Oïdium, and named it after its discoverer, O. Tuckeri. The year following it was ravaging France. In 1850 and 1851 it had spread over Italy and Sicily. In 1852 the Madeira Vines were destroyed by it. It reached Spain and Portugal the same year; and in 1853 at Oporto it enlarged its attacks so much that prayers against the ravages of the disease were offered up in many of the parish churches.

BLEEDING.—We never knew the following plan fail to arrest the bleeding of the Vine:—Cut the face of the wound smooth, and apply a thick plate of iron heated intensely red hot, until that face is completely made black—in short, is reduced to charcoal; then immediately rub in very hard a salve, previously ready, made of two parts tallow and one part fresh quicklime.

VINE TORTRIX (Cochylis or Tortrix vitisana).— We are not aware of its having been noticed in England, though it often does much injury to the Vines in Germany and France.

If the Vines in gardens are examined in April and May, this moth will be seen sitting on the branches; it is most readily observed if the branch is beaten with a stick, when the insect flies out, and soon settles on it again. The female at that season lays her eggs singly on the twigs or buds of the Vine, from which the young are hatched at the time when the blossom-buds are unfolded. These caterpillars fasten several blossom-buds together by means of whitish threads, and eat off the inner parts of the blossoms. When they have finished one part of the bunch of blossoms they proceed to another part, and do the same till the whole bunch is as if covered by a spider's web. The longer the blossom-buds remain small, the greater number of them will be required for the food of the caterpillar; therefore the devastation of this insect will be most felt in cold wet springs. Instances have occurred of trellises, though rich in blossom, not having produced a single ripe bunch of Grapes, all having fallen a prey to these caterpillars.

When fully grown the little caterpillar measures three or four lines, is dirty green, and beset with whitish minute warts, from which arise stiff hairs; the head and first segment of the body are yellowish brown, the six fore feet blackish, and the others the same colour as the body. They enter the pupa state towards the end of June, and appear as moths twelve days afterwards. Pupation takes place either in the cocoon or in a curled-up leaf. The pupa is brown, with rough points.

The moth is three or four lines long, and, with the wings extended, six lines broad. The head is yellowish brown; the antennæ, which are half as long as the whole insect, are black and annulated. The upper wings appear marbled with rust-colour and bluish grey, having two incomplete cross bands of the latter colour, or whitish, in the middle of the first of which, towards the centre, is a dark rusty dot. The second band has several dots and streaks of the same colour, placed irregularly, and a confused whitish mark, which spring from four pairs of little hooks on the anterior edge; the space between the innermost pair is very dark. The under wings are white, with brownish veins and snow-white fringes.

The caterpillars of the second generation of this moth appear towards the end of August and beginning of September, from the eggs of the first. These are also found on the bunches of Grapes but they do less damage, as the berries are then of considerable size. The caterpillar penetrates into them, and feeds on their unripe pulp. When a berry is so much consumed that it begins to wither, its caterpillar spins a round hollow passage, which forms a bridge for its passage into another Grape. Four or five Grapes are sufficient, in general, for the nourishment of one caterpillar; but in rainy weather the mischief extends to a greater number, because those the caterpillar has begun to devour soon rot, and the infection spreads to those near. The fully-grown caterpillar then leaves the bunch of Grapes, to undergo pupation either at the root of the Vine or in some other suitable place. The pupæ of the second generation remain in this state throughout the winter, and it is not till April of the next year that the moths are developed from them.

SCALE.—One of the most common pests of the Grape is the Vine Scale (Coccus vitis). It preys upon the stems and branches of the Grape Vine, both in the open air and under glass. It seems to be the same species which also attacks occasionally the Peach, Nectarine, and Plum. It is, says Mr. Curtis, a longish brown insect, which in old age assumes a blackish brown colour, and becomes hemispherical and wrinkled. The females are shield-like, being convex above, and flat or concave below. They are furnished with six small legs, which, when the insect is old, become part of the substance of the body. On the under side of the insect is a sucker, with which it pierces the cuticle of the plants and extracts their juices. Soon after impregnation the female dies, and her body becomes a protection for the eggs, which are covered with long white wool, and sometimes completely envelope the shoots of the Vines, or of plants growing underneath them. The males are furnished with four wings. Their powers of propagation are immense; and, where they once become very numerous, they are exceedingly difficult to eradicate. This species belongs to the true genus Coccus, characterised by the female having a scale inseparable from her body. While young, both sexes are alike; but the male larvæ pro-

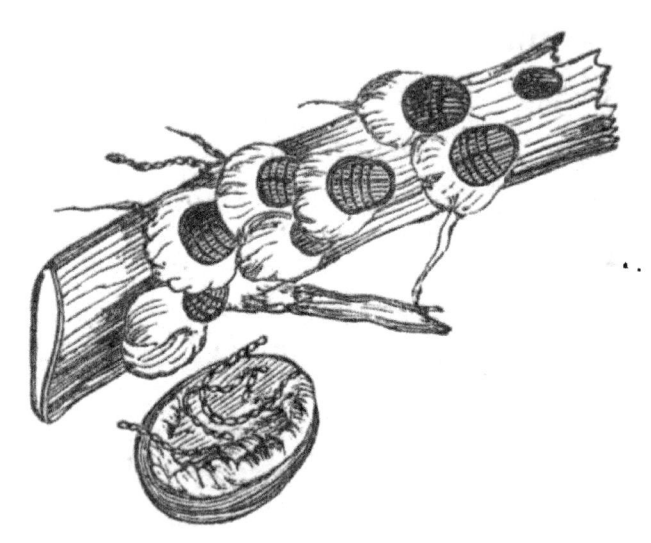

Fig. 32.

duce two-winged insects, with two tail threads. The females have no wings; and their dead bodies, beneath which the young are sheltered, appear as in the annexed woodcut (*fig.* 32).

Whilst the leaves are on the Vine, if any species of scale appears on its stem and branches, the least offensive remedy is to paint over the whole with a strong solution of gum arabic or starch; allow it to remain on for a week, and then wash it off. But the most effectual remedy is to brush them over thoroughly twice after an interval of a day, with spirits of turpentine. To prevent the recurrence of the plague, a very effective mode, in autumn, is to scrape away and burn all the rough bark, and then, with a rough brush, to paint over the stem and branches with a creamy mixture composed of half a pound of soft-soap, one pound of sulphur, and a quarter of an ounce of black pepper, to four gallons of water; boil together for twenty minutes, and make it thick enough to adhere to the wood like paint. If it does not, thicken it with lime, adding sufficient soot to take off the glaring white colour of the lime. The proportions are of little consequence, the object of this and similar washes being by adhering to the wood to prevent the eggs or larvæ of insects from coming to life.

PHYLLOXERA VASTATRIX.—This was not known in England until about two years since.

Its best-known form is that in which no trace of wings can be discovered. When the insect is about to lay its eggs (that is, in its adult female state), it forms a small ovoid mass, having its inferior surface flattened, its dorsal surface convex, being surrounded by a kind of fillet, which is very narrow when it touches the thoracic part of its body, which, formed by five rather indistinct rings, is hardly separated from its abdominal part of seven rings.

Six rows of small blunt tubercles form a slight protuberance on the thoracic segments, and are found very faintly marked on the abdominal segments. The head is always concealed by the anterior protuberance of the buckler; the antennæ are almost always inactive. The abdomen, often short and contracted, becomes elongated towards laying-time, and there can be easily seen one, two, or sometimes three eggs, in a more or less mature state.

The egg sometimes retains its yellow colour for one, two, or three days after it has been laid; more often, however, it changes to a dull-grey hue. From five to eight days generally elapse before it is hatched. The duration of this period depends a good deal on the temperature. The quantity of eggs, and the rapidity with which they are produced, are probably determined by a variety of circumstances—the health of the insect, the quantity of nourishment it is able to obtain, the weather, and perhaps other causes. A female which had produced six eggs at eight o'clock A.M. on the 20th of August, had fifteen on the 21st at four P.M.—that is, she laid nine in thirty-two hours. Other females lay one, two, or three eggs in twenty-four hours. The maximum quantity is thirty in five days. The eggs are generally piled up near the mother without any apparent order, but she sometimes changes her position so as to scatter them all around her. They have a smooth surface, and adhere lightly to each other by means a slimy matter which attaches to them.

Hatching takes place through an irregular and often lateral rent in the egg, the empty and

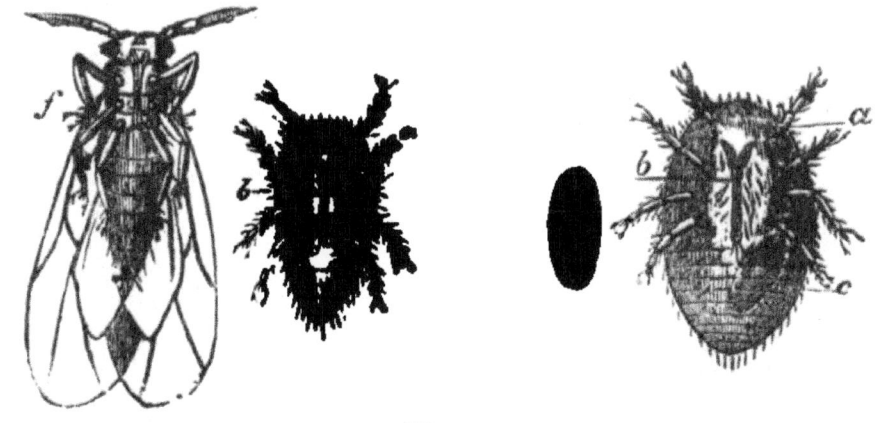

Fig. 33.

Phylloxera vastatrix (J. E. Planchon).—Female specimens and their eggs. *a*, antennæ; *b*, horns or suckers; *c*, egg plainly visible in the body of the insect; *f*, winged form of the insect. All magnified.

crumpled membrane being found among the other eggs in different stages of hatching.

After a few days the young insects seem to fix upon a spot to settle in. Most frequently this is a fissure in the bark of a Vine, where their suckers can be easily plunged into the cellular tissue, full of saccharine matter. If you make a fresh wound on the root by cutting off a little piece of the bark, you may see the "pucerons" range themselves in rows around the wound, and, once fixed, they apply to the root their antennæ, which appear like two small divergent horns. At this period of their life, about the thirteenth or fourteenth day after their birth, they are more or less sedentary; but they change their places if a new wound is made on the root, which promises a fresh supply of food.

It is fortunate that this new enemy to the Vine attacks it in the first instance at the base of the stem, and not underground at the fibres. As it is, a thorough dressing of the bottom of the stem with coal tar will probably prove an insurmountable obstacle to the progress of this destructive insect; but were the case otherwise, it would be very difficult to get down deep enough to reach an enemy so well protected by the depth of the soil.

Weevils.—The Weevil (Otiorhynchus scabrosus) is very destructive to young buds. It feeds by night, and may be easily trapped by laying a cloth beneath the branches by day, and then shaking them about midnight, when the insects are taking their meal. They may be destroyed by sweeping them off the cloth into boiling water. Another little beetle, eater of Vine-leaves, is the Vine Weevil (Curculio betuleti). There is no remedy but holding a sheet under the branches at night, and shaking down from them these little marauders.

Drops on Branches.—Hard and nearly opaque

drops sometimes exude from the bark. This is no disease, but an evidence of the Vine's vigour. Additional air and light are the best applications.

Rootlets on Stems.—The protrusion of these rootlets is evidence that the air of the house has been kept too moist. There is no need for removing the rootlets, but less moisture and more air will prevent their increase.

Going Blind.—Vines are said to "go blind" when the incipient bunches turn up like tendrils, or the flower-buds turn yellow, or droop instead of opening or setting. It is chiefly owing to one of two reasons—1st, want of maturation of wood last season; 2nd, want of relative action between the roots and the branches at the critical period, whether owing to want of heat at the roots, their depth, or over-moist condition. In either case, the Vine, so far as growth is concerned, may seem to be in the highest health; but the fruit will suffer before the leaves, and luxuriance and fruitfulness are not correlative.

# INDEX.

|   |   |
|---|---|
| | Page |
| Admitting Vines from outside borders (*fig.* 2) | 6 |
| Air | 73 |
| | |
| Black Champion Grape | 11 |
| Black Hamburgh Grape | 11 |
| Black Muscat of Alexandria Grape | 11 |
| Bleeding | 126 |
| Blind, going | 135 |
| Borders | 3, 41, 63, 74 |
|     draining | 3 |
|     depth of | 4 |
|     section of (*fig.* 1) | 5 |
|     making bit by bit (*fig.* 3) | 7 |
|     outside covering | 43 |
|     heating (*fig.* 11) | 51 |
|     at Trentham | 6 |
|     for greenhouses | 74 |
|     for stove (*figs.* 15, 16) | 64 |
| Bunches, thinning | 21 |
|     curling | 120 |
|     turning to tendrils | 135 |
| | |
| Calabrian Raisin Grape | 14 |
| Choice of Vines | 10 |
| Coccus vitis | 129 |
| Copings for walls | 101 |

|   |   |
|---|---|
| | Page |
| Curculio betuleti | 134 |
| Cuttings, propagation by | 28 |
| Curate's vinery (*fig.* 26) | 105 |
| | |
| Disbudding | 70 |
| Diseases | 120 |
| Draining borders | 3 |
| Drops on branches | 134 |
| | |
| Early White Malvasia Grape | 13 |
| Eyes, propagation by (*fig.* 8) | 30 |
| | |
| Grape wall-case (*fig.* 24) | 100 |
| Grafting | 33 |
|     cleft (*fig.* 10) | 37 |
|     whip or tongue (*fig.* 9) | 35 |
| Grafting clay | 34 |
| Grafting wax | 33 |
| Greenhouse Vines | 68 |
|     summer and autumn pruning | 68 |
|     winter pruning | 69 |
|     spring management | 70 |
|     summer management | 70 |
| Ground vinery (*fig.* 26) | 105 |

# INDEX.

| | Page |
|---|---|
| Heat for Vines | 79 |
| Heating Vine borders (*fig.* 11) | 49 |
| Heating vineries | 47 |
| | |
| Inarching | 37 |
| Insects, to preserve Grapes from | 73 |
| | |
| Keele Hall, vineries at | 53 |
| | |
| Lady Downe's Grape | 12 |
| Layering | 28 |
| Leaves, shanked | 120 |
|     warted | 121 |
| Lifting and replanting Vines | 23, 117 |
| | |
| Mildew (*figs.* 28, 29, 30, 31) | 123 |
| Mill Hill Hamburgh Grape | 11 |
| Muscat of Alexandria Grape | 11 |
| | |
| Otiorhynchus scabrosus | 134 |
| | |
| Peach-house and vinery combined (*fig.* 14) | 60 |
| Phylloxera vastatrix | 131 |
| Planting (*fig.* 4) | 15, 66 |
|     time of | 9 |
| Pot-culture | 83 |
|     varieties for | 85 |
|     soil for | 85 |
|     young v. old Vines for | 88 |
|     on coiling system (*fig.* 17) | 91 |
| Propagation | 28 |
|     by layering | 28 |
|     cuttings | 28 |
|     eyes (*fig.* 8) | 30 |
|     grafting | 33 |
|     inarching | 37 |
|     seed | 40 |

| | Page |
|---|---|
| Pruning | 17 |
|     greenhouse Vines | 68 |
|     long rod (*figs.* 6, 21) | 19, 96 |
|     spur (*figs.* 5, 23) | 17, 98 |
|     stove Vines | 66 |
| Purple Constantia Grape | 12 |
| | |
| Resting Vines (*fig.* 7) | 22 |
| Ringing (*fig.* 25) | 102 |
| Rootlets on stem | 135 |
| Royal Muscadine Grape | 13 |
| Rust | 122 |
| | |
| Scale (*fig.* 32) | 129 |
| Seed, raising Vines from | 40 |
| Soil and its preparation | 1, 7, 85 |
| Shanking | 120 |
| Shrivelling | 121 |
| Stopping | 69, 70 |
| Spot | 122 |
| Syringing | 72 |
| Stove Vines | 62 |
|     culture of | 62 |
|     borders for (*figs.* 15, 16) | 63 |
|     planting | 66 |
|     summer treatment | 67 |
| | |
| Thinning bunches | 21, 71 |
| Tortrix vitisana | 126 |
| Training | 70 |
|     on walls out of doors (*figs.* 18, 19, 20, 21, 23) | 93 |
| Transplanting | 23 |
| Trentham Black Grape | 12 |
| Trentham, borders at (*fig.* 3) | 6 |
| | |
| Varieties | 11 |
|     selection for vineries | 11 |
|     for forcing | 14 |
|     for stoves | 14, 62 |
|     for greenhouse | 68 |
|     for pot culture | 84 |
|     for walls in open air | 13, 97 |

# INDEX.

| | Page |
|---|---|
| Vineries | 41 |
| early | 74 |
| summer treatment | 74 |
| winter management | 75 |
| summer | 76 |
| winter management | 78 |
| late | 78 |
| summer and winter management | 78, 79 |
| heating | 47 |
| Ground or Curate's (*fig.* 26) | 105 |
| lean-to (*fig.* 12) | 53 |
| span-roofed (*fig.* 13) | 56 |

| | Page |
|---|---|
| Vineries at Keele Hall (*fig.* 12) | 53 |
| at Yester (*fig.* 11) | 49 |
| select Vines for | 11, 12, 13, 14 |
| Vinery and Peach-house combined (*fig.* 14) | 60 |

| | Page |
|---|---|
| Vines, choice of | 10 |
| unpacking and pruning | 10 |
| lifting and replanting | 23, 117 |
| in pots | 83 |
| on trellises | 114 |
| on walls in open air | 93 |
| on walls, pruning and training (*figs.* 18, 19, 20, 21, 22, 23) | 93 |
| Vine-trellises (*fig.* 27) | 115 |

| | Page |
|---|---|
| Walls in open air, varieties for | 14 |
| Walls flued | 100 |
| copings for | 101 |
| Watering | 72, 80 |
| Weevils | 134 |
| West's St. Peter's Grape | 12 |
| White Frontignan Grape | 13 |
| White Tokay Grape | 13 |
| Yester, vineries at (*fig.* 11) | 49 |

Printed at the Horticultural Press, 171, Fleet Street, London.

*A New Volume Commences the First Week in January and July.*

THE
# JOURNAL OF HORTICULTURE,
## COTTAGE GARDENER,
AND
### HOME FARMER
(ILLUSTRATED),

Is the most practical and widely circulating Journal devoted to

## GARDENING IN ALL ITS BRANCHES,

And embracing among other Home Pursuits of the Country House

**POULTRY, BEES, PIGEONS, CAGE BIRDS, &c.**

*Practical Utility rather than ornament is the object of this Old-established Periodical.*

Weekly, 3d.; Post Free, 3½d.

PUBLISHED ON THURSDAY.

*Terms of Subscription, post free:—One Quarter, 3s. 9d.; Half Year, 7s. 6d.; Year, 15s.*

☞ Post-office Orders to be made payable to E. H. MAY.

OFFICE: 171, FLEET STREET, LONDON, E.C.

Printed in Great Britain
by Amazon